TEACHING & CELEBRATING THE CHRISTIAN SEASONS

TEACHING & CELEBRATING THE CHRISTIAN SEASONS

■

A Guide for Pastors, Teachers, and Worship Leaders

Delia Halverson

CHALICE™
PRESS

ST. LOUIS, MISSOURI

Biblical quotations, unless otherwise noted, are from the *New Revised Standard Version Bible*, copyright 1989, Division of Christian Education of the National Council of the Churches of Christ in the United States of America. Used by permission. All rights reserved.

Cover and interior design: Elizabeth Wright
Art direction: Elizabeth Wright

This book is printed on acid-free, recycled paper.

Visit Chalice Press on the World Wide Web at
www.chalicepress.com

10 9 8 7 6 5 4 3 2 1   02 03 04 05 06 07

Library of Congress Cataloging-in-Publication Data

Halverson, Delia Touchton.
  Teaching and celebrating the Christian seasons : a guide for pastors, teachers, and worship leaders / Delia Halverson.
      p. cm.
Includes bibliographical references.
  ISBN 0-8272-3641-7 (alk. paper)
  1. Church year—Study and teaching (Elementary) 2. Worship (Religious education) I. Title.
  BV30 .H34 2003
  263'.9—dc21
                                                              2002007783
Printed in the United States of America

*To all those saints
who have gone before us,
whether known or unknown,
and to those among whom
we live today.*

CONTENTS

INTRODUCTION

I purposely chose not to make this an anthology of seasonal materials. There are many such books on the market for the various seasons of the church year. I hope this book will assist you, as pastor and teacher, in interpreting the seasons to laity of all ages. It will give practical suggestions that you can adapt to each individual situation, such as the suggestion that dramatists develop monologues of specific characters that deal with the particular seasons, ways of developing your own litanies and focus centers for use in the classroom and in worship, and references to particular hymns and special ways to use them.

Most of the chapters of this book take the various seasons and our Sunday experience and suggest opportunities for teaching and celebrating these special times in the life of our church. Because we teach as we celebrate, and we celebrate as we teach, it is important for you to draw ideas from all sections of each chapter, no matter what your role in the church.

At the close of the book are several appendices. One gives sample sentences that you may use in bulletins or newsletters to explain aspects of the worship service and the symbols used in our churches. These may also be used in the classroom to enhance your curriculum. When we understand just why we do certain things in worship, we grow stronger in our spiritual lives.

—1—

WHY FOLLOW THE CHRISTIAN CALENDAR?

I remember the excitement of Christmas and Easter as a child. At Christmas we not only made wishes for special things we wanted, but we planned special gifts for others. We heard familiar stories and even learned our parts in a drama. We sang carols and drank hot chocolate. And the real highlight of Christmas came early on Christmas morning when my dad and the youth group from the church would finish up their early morning caroling right under our window, waking us with the joy of the new day, declaring in song that Christ was born!

During the few days before Easter Sunday we pulled chairs up to the kitchen counter and nervously held the fragile eggs as Mother guided our hands over the hot dye. We waved palm branches and decorated the sanctuary with flowers from neighborhood yards. (We lived in Florida where flowers are in bloom at Easter!) The highlight of the season was the sunrise drama that reenacted the Easter story. Oh, the excitement and anticipation as we watched the story unfold. We knew the end, but it was still a surprise to see that stone rolled away and the risen Christ step from the tomb. And then the choir broke out in song, sounding like angels declaring the resurrection of our Lord!

These were special days, and although I did not yet understand the impact that these celebrated events had on my life (and indeed on the world), I did know that they were significant times. I knew that there was a specialness about them. They were set apart. They had stories that were of prime interest to our church family, and stories that were important within my own family too.

Our church did not celebrate all of the seasons of the Christian calendar. In fact, it was a shock to me each year when many of my classmates came to school on a Wednesday with dark smudges on their faces. More than once I told them they had dirt on their foreheads. The beginning of Lent had gone completely unnoticed in my church family. And now I realize just what a loss that was. What an opportunity was missed for embedding the meaning of Christ's life.

Tradition, Good or Bad

Traditions sometimes get a bad name. Often, when we find a tradition helpful to us, we immediately try to impose that tradition on others around us. Traditions are important because they bring certain things to mind and because they give stability to our lives. Any time that our lives are in upheaval, we immediately lapse into a tradition in order to bring back stability. We saw this especially after the attack on the World Trade Center. There was a resurgence of rituals, families ate meals together more frequently, and the traditions of the seasons took on new meaning. However, traditions can become a vacuum if we have no understanding of why we do them. Without the connection of meaning, when the crisis passes the traditions will fall away.

It is important that we have ownership in our traditions. When someone else's tradition is forced on us, and we have no understanding of it, then it is not meaningful to our lives. When this happens we sometimes push away completely. Or in order to counter the forced tradition and to bring stability, we create our own traditions. This has been evident in the development of what we call contemporary worship. As churches passed down the traditions of ritual, they offered no opportunity for youth and new people to understand and appreciate the worship traditions. It was just expected that they be carried out. Consequently, new expressions of worship were developed which have now become "traditions." Standing during all of the songs and lifting a hand in prayer are examples of these traditions.

History of Special Days and Seasons

The cycle of our Christian seasons brings before us, year after year, the life of Jesus and its impact on the world. Recall a special event, whether an event of joy or of sorrow. The one that comes to mind as I write this is the suicide attack on the World Trade Center on Tuesday, September 11, 2001. On September 12, the morning after the bombing, at the exact time that the first plane hit the first tower, the nation stopped for a time of remembrance. Then a week later, we all paused on that day to offer prayers. When the eleventh day of the next month rolled around, we again offered our prayers for those so impacted by the act, and we honored those who had acted heroically. I daresay that for the rest of our lives, Tuesdays will often cause us to reflect on what happened on that day and how it affected our lives, and the eleventh day of September will be remembered forever in our country. This is similar to the trauma that the early Christians experienced, except theirs had a joyful ending when Christ arose on that Sunday after Passover. And so, even though they continued to worship with the Hebrew faith community, the first day of the week, Sunday, became the natural day for them to pause and remember, and to worship as followers of Christ.

In those early days of Christianity, emphasis was placed on the resurrection because it impacted the true meaning of Jesus' life, and it held such promise for the future. For many years, Easter was the only special day of celebration. This was natural because they were still celebrating the Jewish holy days. In fact, in the earliest Christian writings, Paul's emphasis was on the death and resurrection of Christ. He only mentioned the birth in stating that Jesus was born of woman. The next writings (those of Mark) brought out the baptism of Jesus. The birth of Christ did not seem important enough to mention until Matthew and Luke wrote their gospels. John (the latest of the gospels) pushed the existence of Christ back even further, "In the beginning was the Word, and the Word was with God, and the Word was God" (Jn. 1:1).

As you will see in later chapters, on the foundation of Sundays and the resurrection, additional celebrations were added throughout the centuries, to be repeated year after year. By repeating the cycle, we view the beginning with the end. We see our worship and our understanding of Christ as a yearlong cycle. It becomes richer, because one leads into the next and we see the whole as one.

All Christian churches do not agree on the exact time of the seasons and even some of the seasons themselves. This is especially true of the Eastern Orthodox tradition. Differing calendars and ways of calculating the days and varying historical emphases cause these differences.

Teaching as We Celebrate

Celebrating the various seasons brings new meaning to our worship and removes the distance between the past and the present. That alone would be reason enough for following the Christian year. However, the impact doubles when we recognize the teaching potential of the seasons. Using the church year provides a review of Jesus' life and opportunities to reflect on its meaning to us today. While the Jewish celebrations revolve around the exodus and deliverance from Egypt, the Christian church year focuses on the life and ministry of Jesus.

As early as the OldTestament we find the concept of sacred time as a vehicle for teaching the faith (Ex. 12–13). It is important that this teaching come from the pulpit as well as the classroom.

In the last chapter of Matthew we read that Jesus said, "Go therefore and make disciples of all nations, baptizing them in the name of the Father and of the Son and of the Holy Spirit, and teaching them to obey everything that I have commanded you" (28:19).

In Nehemiah 8 we find the story of the gathering of the community to hear the word, followed by a great celebration. In Jesus' day the synagogue carried on this tradition of gathering to hear the word (Lk. 4:14–21), and the early church adapted this gathering to the first day of the week.Today, some churches have emphasized *only* sermons as "the word" when in fact we grow through many more experiences than just listening.

Jesus commanded us to use teaching in all aspects of our ministry, not just in the Sunday school classroom. Jesus exemplified this in his own ministry. He approached the people using every intelligence with which we learn:

- **Verbal/Linguistic**—has to do with language and words, both written and spoken. *Jesus approached his listeners in this manner with his stories.*

- **Logical/Mathematical**—has to do with inductive thinking and reasoning, statistics, and abstract patterns. *Jesus used questions and answers to reach his listeners who learned this way.*

- **Visual/Spatial**—has to do with visualizing objects and creating internal mental pictures. *Jesus used common objects to explain his meanings to persons who learn in this manner.*

- **Body/Kinesthetic**—related to the physical, such as movement and physical activity. *Jesus involved disciples in learning by fishing and washing their feet.*

- **Musical/Rhythmic**—involves recognition of patterns, both tonal and rhythmic. *Singing hymns was a part of the common experience of Jesus and his disciples.*

- **Interpersonal**—follows relationships between persons, including true communication. *Jesus worked with persons on a personal level and also developed small group settings, his most successful being the twelve disciples.*
- **Intrapersonal**—primarily through self-reflection and awareness of that within us which guides us. *Many times the Bible mentions Jesus drawing away for solitude or to be by himself (or taking his disciples away) for reflection.*
- **Nature**—use of nature in learning. *Jesus used nature in many of his illustrations. He taught in the out-of-doors most of the time.*

Let's look for a moment at how these intelligences can be used as we celebrate the seasons:

- **Verbal/Linguistic**—This is most often used as we explain the seasons through spoken and written word. It is important that some written information about the season be included in the bulletin at each seasonal change. We must assume that there are new persons in our congregation who were not here in previous years and are unaware of the meanings. As we celebrate and worship with litanies and hymns we also teach through this form.
- **Logical/Mathematical**—Sermons offer great opportunities for questions to be posed to worshipers, who will then inwardly reflect on their own answers. Asking open-ended questions forces the worshipers to reflect. Time lines and statistics may also be used for this type of learning. Comparisons, such as the distance from Nazareth to Bethlehem compared to a distance between local cities of today, brings the event into our present world.
- **Visual/Spatial**—Visual representations of the seasons are important. Some people are audio learners, and some are visual learners. In the same manner, some people worship best audibly and some visually. Symbols, paraments, and focal points are excellent ways to enable the visual learner and worshiper. Even the architecture of the gathering place can be used.

- **Body/Kinesthetic**—Just as Jesus used the act of eating the bread and drinking the cup, we also enhance our celebrations by reenacting that last supper that Jesus had with his disciples. Drama engages this type of learning, whether we are in the drama or simply observing it. The body/kinesthetic learning happens when we, as a congregation, stand from time to time in order to express our adoration for God. But the congregation needs to understand that this is the reason that we stand in order for the learning to be effective.
- **Musical/Rhythmic**—This intelligence is one of the most common ones used in celebration of the seasons. Through song and special music we refresh our understanding of Christ's life. Rhythmic litanies or clapping help musical/ rhythmic learners.
- **Interpersonal**—Simply being together as we celebrate is important. Some people believe that we must have a group gathering to have worship. Whether you define worship in that way or not, it is important for a congregation to experience community when they worship together. Reciting creeds and singing together can help with this, and an opportunity in the service for "passing of the peace" builds interpersonal relationship. Study groups are more enhanced if they are small enough for communication between the members, or larger gatherings can be broken down into small groups. There is no law against pausing in the middle of a sermon and asking worshipers to turn to a neighbor and share or discuss something.
- **Intrapersonal**—All too often our worship and our study periods ignore this type of learning. Moments of silent reflection and prayer can be ignored or shortened when we become too time conscious in our worship. Consequently, they need to be built in. I become very frustrated when it's suggested that I pray silently, and then the leader speaks a verbal prayer the whole time. This gives me no opportunity for intrapersonal prayer.

• **Nature**—Most churches use live flowers or plants in their sanctuaries, reminding us of the life-giving power of Christ and reminding us of his resurrection. Congregations need to be made aware that we do not use live flowers just for decoration, but that there is a deeper meaning. We can also enhance this style of learning by making reference to nature in sermons, hymns, and study times.

At-hand Opportunities

Be alert to opportunities at hand for creative ways to celebrate and teach the seasons. Here are a few ideas that some churches have grasped. Your situations will bring about more, if you attune your mind to those opportunities:

Stump from a tree

One church had a tree blow down in a storm. When the stump was removed, they were careful to leave some of the roots intact. They washed the dirt from the tree and saved it for use as a focal point in the chancel. At Advent the tree became the Jesse tree, remembering the reference to the stump of Jesse that would send out shoots (Isa. 11:1–9). The Advent candles were placed among the roots and lit on the Sundays of Advent. At Lent the stump became a symbol for Christ, the root of our faith. The stump might be used at Pentecost or All Saints Day, remembering people of the past who rooted us in the faith.

Barriers broken down

One church enlarged their fellowship hall. After the new addition was built, the old wall between the old and new sections had to be torn down. Before it was destroyed, the congregation gathered in front of the wall and everyone was invited to use paints to draw symbols or write words to describe barriers that we build that separate us from the love of God and that separate us from each other. Then a video and slides were taken of various portions of the wall. Sledgehammers and wrecking bars were brought out, and everyone was invited to begin the destruction of the wall and of the barriers that separate us. More video footage was taken of this act, and of the construction crew's continued destruction of the wall. Then video and pictures were taken as the crew used plaster and paint to repair the place where the old wall was removed, and more pictures and video were taken of the church family celebrating the new fellowship hall. The video and pictures were edited and used on several occasions. They might be used at Lent when we recognize our need to break down barriers that keep us from growing in our faith; during Lent or Easter when we remember how Christ's death broke us free for salvation; at Pentecost when we remember that the Holy Spirit came to unite us and heal the wounds of separation. A piece of the broken wall might be saved to use in the chancel as a focal point during a specific season.

—2—

THE LORD'S DAY

Without the first day of the week, we would not have a differentiation that brings meaning to all of the days of the week. The congregation comes together to worship on the first day of the week, and then we worship in dispersed places on the other days.

The "first day" on which we worship is symbolically the "day" that God created light. God rested on the seventh day, as the writer of Genesis said in telling the creation story. It was on that day that the Hebrews chose to gather for their corporate worship. All four gospels clearly state that Jesus rose from the dead on the morning of the first day of the week. Paul makes references in his writings that lead us to believe that the Christians had adopted the first day of the week as their time to come together. Since many of them continued to follow the Hebrew faith, they probably worshiped in the synagogues on the last day and then came together as Christians on the first day of the week. In 1 Corinthians 16:2 Paul refers to a collection of money on the first day of the week. By the early second century, "Lord's Day" had become a common term for the first day of the week. By the second century, Ignatius, Bishop of Antioch, wrote of ceasing to keep the Sabbath and living by the Lord's Day. The people of Rome dubbed this first day of the week "Sunday," and the Christians adopted the word and compared Christ's rising from the dead to the rising of the sun. When the emperor Constantine became Christian he declared Sunday as a day without work, except for the "countrymen," who were to attend to agriculture.

It has been said that Sunday is in time what sacred places are in space. It is a setting aside to observe the holy and to remember our heritage. Sunday marks all that God has done both in creation and in salvation.

Sunday should set the stage for the rest of our week. In today's world we have been acclimated to looking at Sunday as the end or climax of the weekend and Monday as the first day of the week. This does not lift the day to its proper position, as the beginning and the model for every day of the week. What we practice on Sunday in our relationship with God should be the pattern for the rest of the week.

Age-level Understandings

Young children do not have a good grasp of the concept of time and therefore don't understand the order of the different days of the week, but they can realize that we have a special day when we go to church together to worship and learn about God. The word "worship" is beyond their ordinary language. Perhaps the simplest way of understanding worship is to refer to it as "loving God and showing that love in song and words."

It is important to involve children in corporate worship at an early age. There are almost no other opportunities for all ages to come together in today's world. Young children appreciate doing what the adults do, and there is a "window" up to about grade three or four when they still think it's great to participate in activities with adults. If we get much past that age before introducing them to corporate worship, then we lose them, because they are more interested in the activities of their peers than those of adults.

Because children are usually very visual, families with young children should be encouraged to sit down front in the sanctuary. If you have any doubts about this, try sitting in a pew at a child's eye level and see how inviting it is to see nothing but the backs of heads and the hymnals and offering envelopes in the pew racks! No wonder we have messed up pew racks and scuff marks on the back of pews. Some churches have purchased "booster seats" for young children and have them available at the back of the sanctuary for families to pick up and boost their children to an appropriate eye level.

Children will also participate in the service if they have some knowledge of what's going on. Consider a special training for first through third graders and their parents, helping them to grasp our liturgy. If parents are involved, they are better equipped to help them in the pew. Involve children in special leadership roles in the service. The child sitting in the pew feels more involved in the service when he or she sees another child helping with the service. But be sure that a child in a leadership role in worship knows exactly what to do. Nothing is more embarrassing for children than to do something wrong before a large number of people.

No matter what the age, remember that you will also have youth and adults who have very little knowledge about worship. Some may never have been in a worship service before, or they may have only attended on Christmas or Easter. Periodically pause to explain things from time to time. (See Appendix 1.)

For additional suggestions on ways to introduce God, Jesus, the Bible, prayer, and the church to children and youth, see *How Do Our Children Grow?* by Delia Halverson (St. Louis: Chalice Press, 1999).

Celebrating Sunday

- Create visual imagery in worship using a candle and half-bushel basket propped above the candle; light or candle behind a stained-glass hanging/window; musical instruments (symbolizing that we "make a joyful noise to God" on Sundays).

- Create excitement over each celebration of Sunday. Greet the congregation with some sort of statement about joy over this day and this opportunity to be together in worship.
- Involve the congregation in praise by having the people sing along with the choir in some anthems. This can be done when the anthem has a familiar chorus. Singing with the choir gives the worshipers in the pew an opportunity to be more involved. It also takes away the attitude that the anthem is a performance.
- Use church bells, if your church has them, to let the community know that this is a special day.
- Decorating the worship area with live flowers not only reminds us that Christ lives today, but creates an atmosphere of excitement for the day. Try different types of floral arrangements to call special attention to the day. The flowers might be in a woven basket (symbolizing that the congregation is woven together with God's love), or a crystal vase (symbolizing the clear vision of God's love), or even an earthen crock (symbolizing the strength of God's love). When such symbols are used, make note of them verbally or in the bulletin.
- Have the lights dimmed as the worshipers enter the sanctuary, and then as you sing the first hymn turn on all the lights. Remind the worshipers: "Christ, whom we worship this First Day, is sometimes called the 'dayspring' of life."
- To open morning worship, use songs such as "When Morning Gilds the Skies," "Rise, Shine, You People," "Christ Is the Light of the World," and "Morning Has Broken." Make reference on the bulletin or verbally to the fact that we stand to greet this new Lord's Day with the morning song.
- Display banners at the doors of the sanctuary celebrating the Lord's Day. These banners may have designs of a sunrise or other forms of light.

- During children's moments, talk about the various persons who help to make our celebration on Sundays possible. Include those behind-the-scenes persons such as those who print and fold bulletins, those who straighten up the pew pockets during the week, and those who clean the building. Introduce those persons in the service.
- Ask different families to bake bread for each celebration of communion and then present it at the front at some point during the service. Place the family name in the bulletin. This gives the families involvement in the service and celebrates our church family.

Teaching the Lord's Day

- Make badges saying "Ask me about the Lord's Day" for persons who have learned the meaning of it. These will be worn during this special day.
- Use sentences in the bulletin about aspects of worship to educate the congregation. (See Appendix 1.)
- Create bulletin boards about: Sunday's special events; greeting a new day/Sunday; persons who make Sunday special at church.
- Take show-me trips with children to learn about the sanctuary and experience sitting in the pastor's seat, the choir loft, at the piano/organ. (See Appendix 1 for information about aspects of the sanctuary.)
- Use flat pictures of various celebrations, including worship. Ask each person to take a picture and suppose what the celebration might be about. After each has shared, remind them that the Lord's Day is a celebration. Ask for suggestions of what we celebrate in worship on the Lord's Day.
- Encourage Sunday school classes (adults and youth, as well as children) to study about worship. This might be a series of Sundays when the whole church studies it. Check your denominational listing for such studies.
- Teach often-used hymns and responses in the classroom so that they are familiar.

- Make a recording of several hymns, responses, creeds, and the Lord's Prayer for children to take home and practice with. This can be done by taking recordings from your Sunday service and reproducing a master tape with these on it, using the actual voices of your congregation. The tape can then be duplicated and each child given a tape.

—3—

ADVENT

Although we consider this the first season of the Christian year, the celebration of Advent and Christmas were not the first Christian seasons to be celebrated. Easter was the only seasonal celebration that was specifically Christian for the early church. Since they were expecting the immediate return of Christ, they centered on the resurrection celebration. Then they began to celebrate the coming of the Holy Spirit at Pentecost, which had its roots as a celebration of their Jewish heritage.

Advent and Christmas help people see Jesus as not only a divine being, but a human person who had the same kind of experiences we have. At Christmas we celebrate the birth of a baby to a loving but unknown family, among common animals, and in an inconspicuous village. His birth revealed God as a loving God concerned about the poor and the rich alike, not as a distant untouchable figure of kingly nature.

It may be that the Christmas celebration on December 25 originated in a winter solstice celebration according to the ancient Roman calendar. As Christianity took root in the Roman Empire, Christmas served as a replacement for the existing pagan Festival of the Unconquered Sun, which marked the winter solstice.

Some theologians believe that Christ was born in the springtime, since shepherds were in the fields. However, we have no way of determining exactly when he was born. The rulers of the church set aside the month of December to celebrate, and how appropriate, since it is the darkest and shortest time of the year, known as the season of the winter solstice. After years of rejection and persecution, the Christians moved into a season of new hope, and Christmas became a celebration of new light coming into the world bringing the promise of brighter days and a hope of renewed life, just as the days following the winter solstice.

In 354 C.E., December 25 was established as the birthday of Christ, and in 440 the pope in Rome decreed that Christmas should be celebrated on that day. In the fourth century, Advent was a period of penance and of preparation for baptisms that took place on Epiphany (January 6). In the sixth century, Advent was moved to the four weeks before Christmas Day and a special liturgy was added. In the ninth and tenth centuries, Advent's meaning was broadened to include the expectation of the second coming of Christ.

Purple is the most often used color for Advent, although some churches are now using royal blue. When we use purple during both Advent and Lent we not only declare the coming of Christ as our king at Advent but we also connect this season of anticipation with Lent and Holy Week, the time we remember Christ's suffering for us. When royal blue is used we again symbolize the royalty of Christ. Blue is also a color representing hope. Some churches use a bright blue to symbolize the night sky and the anticipation of the announcement of Christ's coming. It can also represent the waters of creation with Advent as the anticipation of a new creation.

The use of evergreens and holly symbolizes the continuing life and hope that Christ's birth brings, even into a world that seems cold and harsh. Red represents Christ's blood shed for us.

Age-level Understandings

Children sometimes have difficulty with "waiting time" or anticipation of an important event. It helps to have something that moves that waiting along. Advent calendars are a popular tool for this. Each day opens up a new idea or an act that they can do for someone else. The Advent wreath helps them to count off the weeks.

It is easy for children to miss the connection between the Baby Jesus and the grown man Jesus. We can help to make this connection by referring to "when Jesus was a baby" and reminding them of stories of Jesus' manhood during this waiting season. Refer to Christmas as the time when we *remember* when Jesus was born. Explain that Advent is when we get ready for Christmas, and Christmas Day is the day when we celebrate Jesus' birth.

We can also help children realize that we have two names for this man whose birth we celebrate, Jesus and Christ. Older children can learn that Christ means Messiah, or one who comes to save us.

There are many aspects of our Christmas celebrations that are strictly fun and have very little if any connection to the real meaning of the season. We need not remove that from our lives, but it is important to help children recognize the religious significance of the season.

For additional suggestions on ways to introduce God, Jesus, the Bible, prayer, and the church to children and youth, see *How Do Our Children Grow?* by Delia Halverson (St. Louis: Chalice Press, 1999).

Celebrating Advent

- Create visual imagery in worship using these for the various Sundays in Advent:

  1st Sunday—Empty manger
  2nd Sunday—Children come down aisle bringing handfuls of straw

> 3rd Sunday—Youth bring bench for Mary and cloth to wrap baby
> 4th Sunday—Mary and Joseph come in at close of service, but no baby, Mary obviously pregnant
> Christmas Eve/Day—Add baby and shepherds
> Epiphany—Mary, Joseph, baby and wise men—remove manger (see reference to house in Mt. 2:11)

- The Advent Wreath is used in many churches. This is created with four purple candles and the white Christ Child candle in the center, lit on Christmas Eve and/or Christmas Day. A purple candle is lit each Sunday of Advent. Consider these themes for each Sunday:

Creation	Genesis 1:1–5
All people	John 1:9–13; Matthew 2:1–2
Gifts	John 1:14–18, 1 John 4:7–12
Relationship with God	John 14:6–7

Gifts we receive from God:	
Example of Christ	Philippians 2:1–11
New freedom	Galatians 5:1
Free choice	Philippians 1:9–11
Hope	Psalm 33:20–22
Now we give to God:	Matthew 5:14–16

Anticipation	Isaiah 11:1–2
Announcement	Luke 1:26–35
Affirmation	Isaiah 62:10–12
Arrival	Luke 2:1–7
Appreciation	Luke 2:8–20
Christmas Eve (Day)	

- Add visuals to the Advent wreath ritual:

1st Sunday	Hope	Star

2nd Sunday	Faith	Cross
3rd Sunday	Joy	Bell
4th Sunday	Love	Heart
Christmas (Eve)	Peace	Dove
1st Sunday	Prepare our lives	Straw in stable
2nd Sunday	Listen for the word	Angel/shepherd's crook
3rd Sunday	Good news	Bible
4th Sunday	Wise men spread the word	Jewel box
Christmas (Eve)	The light comes at Christmas (Eve)	Oil lamp

- Decorate a Chrismon tree for your sanctuary using various symbols for Christ. Print up the meaning of the symbols on the tree and have the information available in the pews or in a book that is kept near the tree.
- Decorate a Jesse tree. This tree has symbols that explain the heritage of Jesus (Isa. 11:1). Note that women have been used in this list as well as men.

Abraham	Genesis 15:1–6	Star
Sarah	Genesis 21:1–8	Baby
Isaac	Genesis 22:1–14	Altar
Rebecca	Genesis 24:12–20	Water jug
Jacob	Genesis 28:1–22	Stairway
Rachel	Genesis 29:15–20	Number 7
Joseph	Genesis 37:1–4	Coat
Judah	Genesis 37:25–28	Coins
Joseph	Genesis 44:1–17	Cup
Ruth	Ruth 2:1–12	Wheat

Boaz	Ruth 4	Sandal
Jesse	1 Samuel 16:1–13	Sheep
David	2 Samuel 2:1–7	Crown
Solomon	1 Kings 3:1–15	Gavel
Jehoshaphat	2 Chronicles 20:1–12	Praying hands
Hezekiah	2 Chronicles 29:1–11	Gates to Temple
Josiah	2 Kings 22:8–20	Scroll
Joseph	Matthew 1:18–25	Angel
Mary	Luke 2:1–7	Manger
Jesus	Matthew 3:13–17	Dove

- Set up a manger for "Friendly Beasts" in the chancel area. Invite people to bring stuffed animals that will be gifts for children in places such as a home for abused women and their families.
- Have a worship service with "lessons and carols," alternating scripture with Christmas carols.
- *Cristkind* is a German word meaning Christ Child. Recreate an Old World Advent custom by exchanging names of families (households) in your church. Throughout Advent families who have signed up for this pray for the family whose name they received and try to do small acts of kindness for the family without letting them know who is doing it.
- Share nativity crèches as you celebrate. Invite families to bring a favorite nativity set or crèche to be on display on a specific Sunday. Set up the display in a large room and provide cards to be filled out for each display, giving the name of the family and some background about the display. Provide refreshments for the occasion and celebrate Christ's birth.
- To make a point of anticipation or waiting during Advent, use a timer that ticks loudly.
- Purchase or create a devotional booklet to be used for celebration in the homes. You can create one by asking members of the church to write devotionals to be included.

Suggest that each devotional have a key scripture and include a "feeling-into" activity or question, an opportunity to "meet with" the scripture, and a suggestion for a way to "respond to" the scripture. These might include poems, stories, discussion themes, and activity suggestions. Each devotional should include a prayer and scripture.

- Celebrate spiritual gifts by wrapping boxes that contain slips of paper with words on them like love, peace, hope, friendship, joy, happiness, cooperation, goodness, kindness, sharing. Place the gifts attractively at a focal point in the chancel. Unwrap one gift at a time, talking about ways that we can give that particular gift when it is opened. These may be unwrapped all at one celebration or over a period of time.
- Celebrate the season with a baby shower for the Christ Child. Give the gifts to an abuse center, a mission hospital, or families that are in need.
- See "Stump from a tree" on page 10.
- Ahead of time, invite children to come to the service dressed as any character of the Christmas story that they like. Have additional costumes on hand for those who forget or are unaware of the arrangements. As the story is read, when the person enters the story, all children dressed as that character come to the chancel area and take a place. You may have five Marys and only one wise man, but this doesn't matter. The involvement in the story is what is important.
- Every year we sing the Christmas carols over and over. They can become more meaningful to us if we know the stories behind the carols. Each Sunday of Advent, choose a special carol and tell the story behind the writing of the carol.
- Create banners that add to the story. Each Sunday add the next section to what becomes a collage of related banners. By letting the congregation know that an addition will be hung each week, you will help them experience anticipation.
- Build a large nativity scene in the chancel area as the Advent season progresses. Set up the basic structure the first Sunday and ask worshipers to bring items to add to the scene each

week. They might bring rocks, mosses, berries, straw, buckets, blankets, curry comb, and so forth. On the Sunday before Christmas Eve/Day, add the manger, and on Christmas Eve/Day add the Christ Child and any other characters you like.

- Celebrate with a birthday party for Jesus. Bake a large cake and place twelve large candles on the cake. During the celebration light the twelve candles, one at a time. Everyone will be given an opportunity to bring a gift (money or object) for a mission you have selected when a candle is lit for his or her birthday month. When each candle is lit, call out the month and invite those who were born in that month to bring their gift to the Christ Child.

- Use heritage bells. Place a tree in the chancel area, and throughout the Advent season invite persons to bring bells to place on the tree in memory or honor of someone who has been influential in their faith journey. Have a special book near the tree for them to write the name of the person they are honoring. Use the scripture Exodus 28:33–35 and the hymn "I Heard the Bells on Christmas Day."

- Another version of this might be to have bells available at the door when worshipers arrive and ask them to pin a bell on streamers (which are attached to a standard) to honor or in memory of someone who brought the true meaning of Christmas to them. Then the streamers with bells are brought down the aisle during the singing of the first hymn, "I Heard the Bells on Christmas Day."

- Use a strolling actor to tell the story. The actor comes down the aisle, greeting people and saying that he or she recalls the story and then begins to tell it. The story is told from the viewpoint of that character in the story, such as prophet, inn keeper, shepherd, Joseph, Mary, Simeon, or Anna.

Teaching Advent

- Make badges saying "Ask me about Advent" for persons who have learned the meaning of the season. These will be worn during this special season.

- Create bulletin boards to: parallel the themes you use in your Advent candle lighting ceremony; give information and progress for any Advent project you may have; display the journey from Nazareth to Bethlehem and show the progress of Mary and Joseph each week.
- Review anticipation moments by asking each person to share a time when they have waited for a special event or visit from someone, perhaps the first day of school or the visit of a relative. Remind them of the excitement and joy that happens as the time draws near. This is what happens when we celebrate Advent, our time of waiting for Christmas. You might say, "Get your lap ready; something great is going to fall in it!"
- Create a journey to Bethlehem with learning centers for students (all ages) to learn about life in Bethlehem: carpenter shop (make gift from wood); weaving shop (make woven ornament); candle shop (make candle); dye shop (make batik design); gift and card shop (make gift wrap); bakery shop (enjoy pita bread and fruits; grape press; drink grape juice).
- Teach the background of Santa. The original idea came from the story of Saint Nicholas, who loved Jesus and tried to help others as Jesus did. He often performed kind deeds anonymously. Later he became a bishop, and people remember him as a saint because that's what people who love God are called. Check the library for the full story.
- Instead of asking children what they want from Santa, ask questions such as "How are you going to be a 'Santa' for someone else?" This makes giving the central point.
- Make Advent chains. Print up seven suggestions for family activities on a page, dividing them evenly down the page so that they may be cut apart to make links for a chain. Make four pages of these, so that there is one link for every day of Advent. Families will select one activity each day and add it to the chain after they do the activity.
- Give each child a "manger" box and a small bag of straw. When they do a kind act, they take a straw from the bag and place it in the "manger" to prepare the place for the Christ Child.

- Giving trees shift the emphasis from receiving gifts to giving. Set up a Christmas tree in a common area and ask that items be hung on the tree. These may be mittens, caps, toiletries, school supplies, or toys. Another version of this is an "Angel Tree," where paper angels are placed on the tree with names and sizes of recipients written on the angels. A family takes an angel and purchases gifts for the person and then brings the wrapped gift back to the tree, placing the angel information on the outside of the gift.
- Teach youth a different type of giving. Raise money in some way, and then plan a time for the youth to take deprived children on a shopping trip so that the children can buy gifts that they can give to their own family members.
- To encourage better understanding of Christmas carols, print the words on a poster board or large paper and ask students to illustrate the words with pictures on the edges of the poster.
- Use old Christmas cards or pictures from advertisements to spark conversations about the true meaning of Christmas. Or you may ask for words that tell about the true meaning of Christmas, printing these on a bulletin board (joy, gifts, peace, nativity, wise men, shepherds, etc.). Then hand out the old cards and pictures and ask students to post them under the appropriate words.
- Supply your classrooms with individual nativity sets by making one for each class out of wood. Then give each set to an "artist" in your church, asking them to paint the clothing and features on the figures. Print the name of the artist on the back of each piece. On the first Sunday in Advent have a display of the art work and thank the artists. Then place them in the classroom. Be sure to store these sets carefully between seasons to preserve the artists' work.
- Study Advent and Christmas celebrations from other countries using the theme: Christ Came for All.
- Study the parable of the bridesmaids (Mt. 25:1–13) and compare the anticipation of the bridesmaids with our anticipation of Christmas.

- Create Advent calendars for use in the home. This might be a drawing of a tree with ornaments and gifts. On each ornament or gift print a suggestion of a kind act that a person might do as a gift to the Christ Child. When the act is done, that ornament or gift is colored in. By Christmas the calendar is complete. For other years, make the calendar into a quilt with each act written on a quilt piece.
- Set up an experiential learning "Journey to Bethlehem." This walk-through learning can have ten sections with appropriate scenes set up: prophecy, annunciation, Joseph's dream, journey, entering Bethlehem, the inn, shepherds, angels, manger, and wise men. In warmer climates this is done as a "Drive-Through Christmas Story."
- Visit a farm. After you have enjoyed the animals, move into the barn and dramatize the birth story in the barn setting. Older children and adults can grasp the understanding that the humble circumstances of Christ's birth help us to see that Christ came for all people, no matter the circumstances in their lives.
- Decorate the church with greens that were cut in a service project of pruning trees and bushes in yards of people who cannot do yard work themselves.
- Plan an Alternative Christmas Market where people can purchase items for missions. Check with Heifer Project or other mission organizations to determine the cost of donating an animal or some household item or food for a child for a day. Make up cards stating: "_____ has given _____ (animal, seeds, etc.) to those in need in your name." These are then sold and given as gifts. You might even provide gift boxes for the purchasers to use for the cards. If an animal is given, provide a small plastic animal. If seeds, include a replica of a seed package or a miniature spade.

    You might also check out Alternative Gifts International (www.altgifts.org) 800-842-2243—P.O. Box 2267, Lucerne Valley, CA 92356 altgifts@sisp.net.

—4—

CHRISTMAS

The Christmas season begins on Christmas Eve and continues for the twelve days until Epiphany (January 6). Christmas Eve is usually considered part of Christmas. This tradition comes from the adaptation of the Jewish time frame for days. For the Jewish faith, the day lasts from sundown to sundown, and so consequently Christmas Eve would be the beginning of Christmas Day.

Commercially we have such emphasis on Christmas during the month before the actual day that the days following Christmas become a letdown. It is appropriate to continue giving Christmas greetings during this time. Some churches have planned opportunities for children to learn and celebrate the childhood of Jesus during this time frame when they have vacation from school. The decorations should remain, to remind us that we are still in the Christmas season.

Some traditions in other countries place more emphasis on these twelve days than on the days before Christmas. In the section below on teaching Christmas, you will find information on how these twelve days were originally used for learning tools.

31

See the information under "Advent" in chapter 3 for more information on the beginnings of our celebration of Christmas.

Age-level Understandings

Young children have little concept of time and of the development from childhood to adulthood. Unless we speak of Christmas as the celebration of *when* the man, Jesus, was a baby, they are likely to see the baby Jesus and the adult Jesus as two different persons. We need to introduce the adult Jesus to children along with the baby, reminding them that the baby grew up to be an adult who showed us what God is like.

For additional suggestions of ways to introduce God, Jesus, the Bible, prayer, and the church to children and youth, see *How Do Our Children Grow?* by Delia Halverson (St. Louis: Chalice Press, 1999).

Celebrating Christmas

- Create visual imagery in worship using: items representing a stable setting (wool, burlap, straw, etc.); a crèche; baby blanket as altar cloth; candles; symbols of the season.
- During the summer, take pictures of children in scenes from the Christmas story, and then use slides or a PowerPoint presentation to tell the story on Christmas Eve.
- Ask each family to bring a candle in a candleholder. As they enter ask them to light a candle from the Christ Candle and place it on the altar or the altar rail. At the close of the service, the family will carry the lighted candle out and then take the candle with them to use in the home, remembering that Christ has come into their homes. (They may choose to extinguish the light before getting into the car.)
- For a Christmas Eve service, make recordings of children and youth telling the Christmas story as they remember it. Then edit the recordings so that you have one telling of the story, using several voices. Create a slide presentation to accompany the recorded story by taking pictures of scenes around town, including various nativity displays, lighted stars,

people's faces, and so on. A digital camera and PowerPoint work well for this. Add other pictures from Internet sources as needed to create the story. Use plenty of pictures, using several during each section of the story, moving through them fairly quickly to keep interest.

- See "strolling actor" under Advent on page 26.
- Have a "blessing of our gifts" on Christmas day. Ask everyone to bring some representation of a gift that they feel they have received from God. These might be placed at a designated place in the chancel area, around the Christ candle (which represents our greatest gift). During the service have a special time of thanks for these gifts. Provide paper and pencil for persons who didn't bring anything so that they may write their gift on paper and place it with the others.
- Give each person a sprig of evergreen, reminding them that God's love is everlasting, as exhibited by Christ.

Teaching Christmas

- Make badges saying "Ask me about the Christmas Season" for persons who have learned the meaning of the season. These will be worn during this special season.
- Create bulletin boards with symbols of the season; gifts representing all that God gives us in the world; pictures of the nativity from different cultures; many faces of all ages and cultures with the manger and Christ child in the center.
- See "Teaching Advent" on page 26 for suggestions about Santa.
- The origin of the Twelve Days of Christmas was actually a device to teach Christianity. The meaning behind the song is:

True Love	God
Me	Baptized Christian
Partridge in pear tree	Jesus (a partridge acts as decoy to save its babies)
Two turtle doves	Old and New Testaments, witnesses of God

Three French hens	Faith, Hope, Love (1 Corinthians 13:13)
Four calling birds	Four gospels (Matthew, Mark, Luke, John)
Five gold rings	Torah of Old Testament (first five books)
Six geese a-laying	Six days God created (Genesis 1)
Seven swans a-swimming	Seven gifts of Holy Spirit (Romans 12:6–8; 1 Corinthians 12:8–11)
Eight maids a-milking	Eight Beatitudes (Matthew 6:3–10)
Nine ladies dancing	Nine gifts of Holy Spirit (Galatians 5:22)
Ten lords a-leaping	Ten Commandments (Exodus 20:1–7)
Eleven pipers piping	Eleven faithful apostles (minus Judas Iscariot)
Twelve drummers drumming	Twelve points in Apostles' Creed

—5—

EPIPHANY

The word *epiphany* means to go forth. The wise men set out on their epiphany, searching for the Christ Child. When they left to return home, they went forth, spreading the good news to other countries.

If you read the scripture about the wise men carefully (Mt. 2:1–12), you will see that many of the traditions we have about the wise men are only traditions and not facts. We do know that they brought three gifts: gold, frankincense, and myrrh. But there is no reference to an exact number of men. There is no reference to names, although we have adopted the names Balthazar, Caspar, and Melchior. We also have no information about exactly where their journey started. Most scenes of the nativity include the wise men with the shepherds, but the scripture actually says the wise men "entered the house," which implies that it was some time later, when the family was able to move into a house. Because we later read that Herod ordered the boy babies below two years of age to be killed, and if the wise men traveled a distance after they saw the star, we believe that Jesus might have been somewhere between several months of age and age two at the time of their visit.

Some cultures place more emphasis on Epiphany than on Christmas Day and celebrate by giving gifts at this time instead of Christmas.

Age-level Understandings

All of the details of this season, what is factual and what is tradition, will not be as important to children as the simple celebration of how people from other lands learned about Christ's birth. Help them realize that Christ came for all people, no matter where they live or what their background.

For additional suggestions for ways to introduce God, Jesus, the Bible, prayer, and the church to children and youth, see *How Do Our Children Grow?* by Delia Halverson (St. Louis: Chalice Press, 1999).

Celebrating Epiphany

• Create visual imagery in worship using:

three crowns	Symbolizing the wise men
crown	Symbolizing Christ, as king
brick painted gold, oil lamp, and vase	Symbolizing gold, frankincense, myrrh
candles and lamp	Symbolizing Christ as light to the world
star	Jesus' life guides us
map or globe	Symbolizing the spread of the message
Moravian star (many faceted)	No symbolism is officially attached to this star, but we can use it as a symbol of the spread of the message throughout the world

• Use the theme of light and symbol of the star, reminding people that we must follow the light of Christ as the wise men followed the light of the star to Bethlehem.

- Follow the South American custom of placing bales of hay outside the door for the camels of the wise men.
- Begin your service outside, where you burn the Christmas greens. From the burning greens, light the Christ candle. Then have wise men, in robes, come out of the crowd asking, "Have you seen the child that was supposed to be born?" Answer them: "Will you come with me?" Take the candle and lead the wise men and the whole congregation into the sanctuary and begin the service.
- Use a strolling actor to tell the story. The actor comes down the aisle, greeting people and saying that he or she recalls the story and then begins to tell it. The story is then told from the viewpoint of the wise man, Mary, or Joseph.

Teaching Epiphany

- Make badges saying "Ask me about Epiphany" for persons who have learned the meaning of the season. These will be worn during this special day.
- Create bulletin board with gifts. On each gift write gifts of love that we bring to Christ and that we give to each other.
- Research the scripture for passages about stars, remembering that the star led the wise men to Jesus.
- Develop a troupe of traveling wise men. Each person researches what the wise men might have encountered on their journey (how to care for camels, the star locations, terrain of the journey, various foods for such a trip, etc.). You may even make maps. Each wise man then develops a might-have-been-story about the journey. Then they dress in costume and visit classrooms. The wise men may even give out dried fruit, which would have been a food staple for the trip. Each class can leave some hay beside the door for the camels of the wise men. After telling the story and answering questions, the wise man invites the class to come to the sanctuary (or another designated place) and visit the Christ Child.

—6—

SEASON AFTER EPIPHANY

This season begins on January 7 and lasts until Ash Wednesday. The length of the season varies, depending on the date of Easter (determined by the full moon and the spring equinox). Some churches call this and the season after Pentecost "Ordinary Time." This does not mean mundane or common, but rather comes from the word *ordinal,* which means, simply, counted or chronological time, the time in order. Lectionary themes may be used during these times, and we also emphasize the life and teachings of Jesus. Another theme is to look at the spread of the gospel in all parts of the world, following the example of the wise men.

Age-level Understandings

We can use this season to help children grasp the connection between the baby Jesus, whose birth we celebrate at Christmas, and the adult Christ, who later gives his life for us. This is a time for them to learn of the many aspects of Jesus' life and teachings.

For additional suggestions for ways to introduce God, Jesus, the Bible, prayer, and the church to children and youth, see

How Do Our Children Grow? by Delia Halverson (St. Louis: Chalice Press, 1999).

Celebrating the Season after Epiphany

- Create visual imagery in worship using: fish and fishnets (symbolizing any time in Jesus' life when he was fishing or when he spoke of fishing); water, shells, dove (symbolizing Jesus' baptism); stones, seeds, pearl, coins, sheep, and other items representing the parables.
- Use a guided imagery journey to tell a story about Jesus' life. As the "guide" begin something like this: "You are walking on a hot, dusty road in Galilee when the wind brings a scent of water. As you look up you see a hint of blue in the distance. It must be the Sea of Galilee!"
- Use a strolling actor to tell about a section of Jesus' life or a parable. The actor comes down the aisle, greeting people and saying that he or she recalls the story and then begins to tell it. The story is then told from the viewpoint of some character in the story, such as a disciple, someone healed, or some bystander.

Teaching the Season after Epiphany

- Create bulletin boards with different stories from Jesus' life or his parables portrayed.
- Create a time line of Jesus' life.
- Learn of the Hebrew traditions and customs for young men that Jesus would have followed as he grew up.
- Study about the early church missions, particularly those that spread to the east in the land of the wise men.
- Learn about where the message of Christ has spread.
- Use the great "I am" statements from Jesus:

John 6:35	Bread
John 8:12	Light
John 10:7–10	Gate
John 10:11–15	Good shepherd

John 15:1	Vine
John 14:6	Way
John 11:25–26	Resurrection and life

Remember that "I am" is the name that God told Moses to use for God (Ex. 3:1–14).

—7—

LENT

Lent is a forty-day period of preparation for the highlight of our celebrations, Easter. It begins on Ash Wednesday and ends with the Easter service. The forty days do not include Sundays. In the past, Lent was observed with very strict fasting, and so the Sundays, which are considered mini-Easters or "feast days," cannot be included. In reality, the period of Lent includes forty weekdays and six Lord's Days.

The number forty is a popular number in the Bible and is a round number used to represent fullness.

- The rain fell on Noah's ark for forty days.
- Forty days was the required time for embalming when Joseph died.
- Moses and Elijah both lived in Horeb for forty years (at different periods).
- The Israelites wandered for forty years before coming into the promised land.
- Twice Moses was on the mountain for forty days.
- Israel was at peace during the last forty years of Gideon's life.
- Goliath challenged the Israelite army for forty days before David killed him.

- The kings Saul, David, Solomon, and Joash were reported to have ruled for forty years each, and Eli was judge over Israel for forty years.
- Ezekiel predicted that Egypt would lie in ruins for forty years.
- The Hebrews were in exile for forty years.
- Jesus fasted forty days in the wilderness.
- After the resurrection, there was a forty-day period when Jesus was revealed to the disciples.

The number forty indicated an amount of time essential for accomplishment of what needed to be done. And so forty days were set aside for converts to make their special preparation for baptism, which would take place on Easter Sunday. Whether before or after baptism, these forty days of repentance and renewal were representative of Jesus' time of preparation in the wilderness.

Although Holy Week is actually a part of the Lenten season, I have placed suggestions for Holy Week in a separate chapter. See page 53.

Purple is the color associated with Lent. Purple represents royalty and penitence. In preparing to meet our King, we recognize ourselves as unworthy and in need of repentance. Therefore, purple reminds us to take inventory of ourselves in preparation for Easter.

We begin the season with Ash Wednesday. The ashes are placed on the forehead, representing our mortality. But they are placed in the sign of the cross, reminding us that as Christians we die in Christ. As we move through the season, we move from despair to hope, as Good Friday offers redemption with Christ's death.

To prepare, many people choose to "give up" something during this period so that they can be ready for the full meaning of Easter. It is a time of renewal of our baptism vows, and with that understanding we may also decide to add some special act to our routine. Forty days is a good amount of time to establish an affirmative habit. Others may choose to find some act of kindness that they will do each day for someone else during the forty days, such as writing a note of appreciation for some kind act to someone who normally does not receive thanks.

Long periods of fasting were emphasized in the past, and this does alert us to the meaning of the season. But whether we fast or not, prayer and meditation and reflection on the meaning of Easter are central for Lent.

Age-level Understandings

For young children, forty days is a long time. Their understanding of Lent comes as a time of remembering Jesus and the way that he taught us to live. With repentance comes a turning to the right way of living, and so with children we stress the importance of finding something positive to do during this time. This is not to say that they cannot deal with repentance, but their repentance needs to be specific in nature instead of a general concept of penance. When there is a specific occasion for repentance, they can be reminded that Lent is a special time when we want to tell God that we are sorry. Since their minds have not yet grasped the abstract, they do not have our ability to grasp the true meaning of our "sinfulness." Instead, they will relate "sinfulness" as meaning that they are bad and unloved. The love of God, as shown through Christ, is the heart of Christianity, and they must be well established in that from an early age. As their grasp of the abstract develops they will begin to understand "sinfulness."

Although we do not take part in "new life" rituals for springtime, we can lay a foundation for an understanding of a new life in Christ by stressing new life with preschoolers. Talk about how the whole world is just waiting for new life.

For additional suggestions for ways to introduce God, Jesus, the Bible, prayer, and the church to children and youth, see *How Do Our Children Grow?* by Delia Halverson (St. Louis: Chalice Press, 1999).

Celebrating Lent

- Create visual imagery in worship using: basin and towel (service to others), icons of Christ, path or road (Lent is our way to the cross), praying hands (preparing through prayer), six candles (the six "Lord's Days" before Easter.
- Through the Sundays in Lent use these themes and visual images, adding one each Sunday:

Called to follow	Palm branches
Called to servanthood	Basin and towel
Called to overcome greed	Moneybag
Called to community (communion)	Wheat stalks and grapes
Called to endure suffering	Crown of thorns
Called to the cross	Crude cross
Called to joy(Easter)	Easter lily with ring of candles

- Ashes may be made for Ash Wednesday by burning the Christmas tree or greens from the previous Christmas. Or you may wish to use ashes from some sort of past event such as palms from Palm Sunday or prayers written at a prayer service. If the ashes are made from something specific, make note of that in the service.
- Plan a Lenten wreath lighting service similar to that used during Advent. To do this, use five purple candles, one pink candle, and one large white candle. The wreath may be made from pink and purple ribbons. On the first Sunday light all candles and during the meditation extinguish one purple one. During the second Sunday light all candles and extinguish two, and so on until Easter when they are all lit and remain lighted. Use the pink candle on Palm Sunday and the white one on Easter.
- Keep a live Christmas tree in the sanctuary, and at the beginning of Lent during worship have someone carry a

rustic cross into the altar area and place it near the evergreen (symbolizing how Easter makes eternal life possible). Conclude the service outside, planting the tree on the church property.

- Place your dead Christmas tree in the chancel area, and during the singing of a hymn or anthem have someone use garden clippers to cut off the dead branches. Then have someone saw the top third of the trunk off and then lash it to the bottom two-thirds, forming a cross. Drive a large nail into the top of the cross and place a crown of thorns on it. Drape the cross beams with white fabric. This fabric may be changed to black for a Good Friday service.
- Celebrate with a Pax Cake Service, traditional from tenth century England. The word *pax* is Latin for peace. Pax cakes are like small pancakes. As each cake is eaten, make a suggestion for someone that the people may need to forgive (a member of their family or a friend with whom they have quarreled) or suggest that they repent of some negative thought or act they have committed.
- Wax sprouting onions instead of coloring eggs. These keep longer than eggs and can be enjoyed throughout Lent. Place cans of colored wax (use crayons to color wax) in a pan with boiling water. Dip onions into wax several times to coat desired hue.
- Bring barren branches into the sanctuary, place them in water, and force them to bud early. They remind us of how our faith grows through nourishment during Lent.
- Plan communion or a Lenten service once a week. If your church is in a business community, invite those working in the area for a service early in the morning, at noon, or immediately after work.
- See "Stump from a tree" on page 10.
- See "Barriers broken down" on page 10.
- As you use stories during Lent, consider using a mime with a reader. The mime will use deliberate movement, but no words, to amplify the story as the reader reads it.

- Celebrate with a "Phos Service," which means "The Light." This service is reminiscent of the Greek Orthodox tradition where a member of the household carries the light home from the church. Use a large white candle and carve a cross on the side of it. Announce this ahead of time and have families/individuals sign up to take part in the ritual. On the first Sunday in Lent (or Ash Wednesday) light the candle during the service. At the close of the service the first family/ household on the list takes the candle home to use for a day. The next day they pass it on to the next family/household on the list, and they to the next, and on down the list during Lent. If you run out of names, begin the cycle again.
- Celebrate Lent with your senses. On Ash Wednesday and the different Sundays of Lent give the following items with instructions and scripture to individual members/families in the congregation with the accompanying instructions:

  1. Printed version of a favorite hymn (Mk. 14:26)—They sang a song and went out—Remember songs you have sung during Lent and Easter in past years.
  2. Strip of leather (Jn. 18:12–14)—Wrap the leather strip around your wrists and imagine how it must have felt.
  3. Large thorn or piece of thorny branch (Mk. 15:16–20)— Feel the thorn and remember what Christ endured because he would not back down on his beliefs.
  4. Piece of bark or rough wood (Lk. 23:26)—Imagine how Simon of Cyrene must have felt as he carried the cross for Jesus.
  5. Large nail (Jn. 19:16–18) (In the service, during a silence, have someone pound a nail into wood.)—Imagine that you were at the scene and heard the nails being pounded into Christ's hands and feet.
  6. Cotton swab (Mk. 15:23)—As you leave, dip a cotton swab into the bowl of vinegar and taste it. Take the cotton swab home to remember that although Jesus' death was painful, he felt the pain for us instead of taking the painkiller used in that day.

7. Small bag of spices (Mk. 16:1–8)—Smell the spices and remember how the women took spices to the tomb to use to cover the smell of the decaying body that they expected to find.

8. Candle (2 Cor. 4:4)—Remember that the candle brings light to darkness just as Christ brought eternal light to a dark world. Remember this light in the dark times of your life.

- Purchase or create a devotional booklet to be used to celebrate in the homes. You can create one by asking members of the church to write devotionals to be included. Suggest that each devotional have a key scripture and include a "feeling-into" activity or question, an opportunity to "meet with" the scripture, and a suggestion for a way to "respond to" the scripture. These might include poems, stories, discussion themes, and activity suggestions. Each devotional should include a prayer.

Teaching Lent

- Make badges saying "Ask me about Lent" for persons who have learned the meaning of the season. These will be worn during this special time.
- Create bulletin boards throughout the season with themes of the various events in Jesus' last days.
- On Ash Wednesday or the first Sunday of Lent, give out journal pages you have prepared:

When I've seen God in another person's life

When I've seen God in nature

When I've felt God was urging me to do a loving act

Each Sunday offer an opportunity for those who would like to share an entry they've made in their journal that week.

- Lent is a time to look at our own "wilderness wanderings" or our temptations and failures. We need to recognize positive and negative peer pressures and realize that Jesus had human qualities too, and so he experienced much of what we experience.

- Eat/make pretzels, which remind us of arms folded in prayer. In early days the bread was known by its Latin name, *bracellae* or "little arms." That name became "bretzel" and then pretzel. This bread was prepared for use during Lent.
- Prepare Passover foods, remembering that Jesus and his disciples ate the Passover meal as their last supper. Part of that meal is now used as our communion, a way of remembering Jesus.
- Distribute Lenten calendars. These can be purchased or made by your church. They may use various scriptures or prayers, or they may have suggestions of acts of kindness that may be done each day.
- Use the story of the "Forgiving Father" (Lk. 15:11–32) with a discussion of repentance and forgiveness.
- See "Celebrate Lent with your senses" on page 48.
- See "Use the great 'I am' statements" on page 40.
- Too often we forget that to prepare to celebrate means to practice. It's legitimate to celebrate the resurrection during Lent because we are practicing for Easter. We learn about what we will be celebrating as we get ready to celebrate.

—8—

HOLY WEEK

We often combine Holy Week and Easter Sunday, because the understanding of one depends so heavily on the other. In fact, when we work with children, we never tell the first part of the story without including the joyful ending. After all, this is the crux of our religion. They go together.

However, by putting these together, we combine two actual seasons of the church year. Holy Week is a part of the season of Lent, and Easter begins on Easter Sunday and extends to Pentecost.

Holy Week includes Palm Sunday, Maundy Thursday, and Good Friday. Palm Sunday helps us remember when Christ rode into Jerusalem on a donkey or ass. When kings came to a city in war, they rode a horse. When they came into a city in peace, they rode an ass. By his actions, Christ came into Jerusalem as a king in peace.

Some churches choose to call the Sunday before Easter "Passion Sunday" to celebrate the beginning of Jesus' agonizing journey to the cross. Passion comes from a Latin word that means "to suffer." This is the same word that is the root of our word "patient." Many churches include a taste of Christ's suffering in this Sunday experience for those who cannot be a part of the Good Friday service. Since it is Sunday, and all Sundays are celebrations of the resurrection, such a service should not end on a mournful note.

On Thursday of Holy Week we celebrate Maundy Thursday. The word "maundy" comes from the Latin word *mandatum*. This is the same word that is the root of our word "mandate." The Latin word means to entrust or to order or command. In John 13:34–35, we learn that after the meal, Jesus gave his disciples a "new commandment," to love one another so that people would know that they were his disciples. The arrest of Jesus after his meal with his disciples was actually on Friday, according to the Jewish custom of counting days from sundown to sundown. Therefore any remembrance of that arrest comes on Friday.

Friday of Holy Week is called Good Friday. We can call it good, because we live on the Easter side of that day. We know the outcome and know just what Christ went through for us, and so it is a Good Friday for us. This is a time to reflect on the suffering of Christ, building the contrast between Jesus' death and the resurrection. We cannot fully appreciate the resurrection until we have gone through the suffering. This service usually ends on a negative note, and so churches usually don't celebrate communion at this service.

Our Easter celebration has become an adaptation of many rituals from other religions, but the meaning is central to our faith. See the introduction to the next chapter for more information on this.

Age-level Understandings

Young children cannot grasp the abstract meaning of Christ's dying for us, and so this is a week when we read stories with young children about Jesus and talk about "When Jesus grew up and became a man." Of course young children will hear about the death of Jesus, and they can repeat what we tell them about the death, but they will not grasp the full meaning until late elementary or teen years.

We should be careful not to place the blame for Jesus' death on the Jews. Jesus himself was a Jew. It was his enemies, or those who didn't believe what he was teaching about God, who killed him.

When we teach children about Maundy Thursday, we remember that this was a day when Jesus ate a special meal with his friends. We have a celebration that we call the Last Supper, communion, or the eucharist, that helps us remember that.

Children need to understand that we call Friday "Good" because we know the Easter side of the story. We know that God didn't let Jesus stay dead. We use an empty cross because we know that Jesus is no longer dead. Older children can understand that crucifixion was a common way of putting people to death in that day. Those convicted were hung on a cross until they died. When we tell children about the crucifixion we should always accompany it with the story of the resurrection.

Young children can understand that the cross "reminds us of God's love in a special way." Elementary children can understand that the cross "tells us that God's love is greater than any wrong we may do." Older elementary children can begin to grasp that "Jesus could have avoided the cross, but he stood up for what he believed about God."

For additional suggestions for ways to introduce God, Jesus, the Bible, prayer, and the church to children and youth, see *How Do Our Children Grow?* by Delia Halverson (St. Louis: Chalice Press, 1999).

Celebrating Holy Week

- Create visual imagery in worship using: palms and blankets that might have been spread in Jesus' path, bread and cup, rustic cross, large hammer and large spikes, old fence post with rusted spikes in it. (Reflect on how it is like Good Friday.)

- On Palm Sunday, spread palm branches on the floor throughout the church building, not just in the sanctuary.
- On Palm Sunday, provide a basket of palm branches at the door of the sanctuary and invite worshipers to take a palm branch and spread it in the aisle, preparing the way for Christ. Scarves of fabric might also be used in this manner.
- On Palm Sunday have the children bring palm branches in and place them on the floor in front of the altar table. At one point during the service, have each person write on a card something he or she wishes to praise God for. Then during a hymn, have them bring the cards down and lay them on top of the palm branches. Follow this action with the singing of a praise song.
- Give each person a cross made from palm strips on Palm Sunday.
- Plan communion or a brief prayer service each day during Holy Week. If your church is in a business community, invite those working in the area for a service early in the morning, at noon, or immediately after work.
- Use the trunks from your Christmas/Chrismon trees and make a rustic cross for Good Friday.
- Plan a Seder meal for the congregation, similar to what Jesus and his disciples would have experienced. For information see Christian Resource Institute, www.cresourcei.org. or www.crivoice.org
- During a service, have someone sit in the chancel area and form a crown of thorns, using garden gloves to protect the hands. Place this on the altar or a cross. This might be done during the singing of a hymn such as "O Sacred Head, Now Wounded" or "To Mock Your Reign, O Dearest Lord."
- Reenact the scene of Jesus washing the disciples' feet in simple form, or perhaps in mime.
- Use a strolling actor to tell the story. The actor comes down the aisle, greeting people and saying that he or she recalls the story and then begins to tell it. The story is then told from the viewpoint of some character in the story, such as a disciple, centurion, or someone in the courtyard during the trial.

- See "Stump from a tree" on page 10.
- See "Barriers broken down" on page 10.
- Create a service to remember the events of Holy Week and Easter Sunday by interviewing the following persons (actors) and their involvement in the events:

    Person renting room to disciples

    Gardener at Gethsemane

    Serving girl and Peter

    Pilate

    Simon of Cyrene

    John as he stood with Jesus' mother at the foot of the cross

    Joseph of Arimathea

    Centurion at the tomb

    Mary or Salome

    Peter

    Cleopas on the road to Emmaus

    Thomas

- Nails in a Cross: In a service to remember the reactions of various people during the last hours of Christ, use six large spikes that will be nailed into a wooden block or cross at specific times of silence during the service. These may be times of remembering:

  1. Betrayal by Judas
  2. Jesus' request of the disciples to pray and their falling asleep instead
  3. Authorities' arrest of Jesus
  4. Peter's denial
  5. Crowd's shout, "Crucify him!"
  6. Rejection of Jesus by one of the thieves crucified beside him, but affirmation of him by the other. (Ask, "Which will you do?")

- Tenebrae Service—the word *tenebrae* is a Latin word meaning "shadows." In this service we move from light to darkness.

At the close of the service all paraments and other articles are removed from the chancel except the Bible and cross, with a few more lights turned off when each item is removed. The cross is draped in black and then suddenly the Bible is slammed shut (symbolizing the closing of the tomb), and the final lights go out. Sit briefly in silence and darkness, and then raise enough lights for people to exit.

- For a Good Friday service, use the traditional scriptures that cover the seven last words (statements) of Christ.

Father, forgive them…	Luke 23:34
Today you will be with me in Paradise…	Luke 23:43
Woman, here is your son…	John 19:26–27
My God, my God…	Matthew 27:46; Mark 15:34
I am thirsty.	John 19:28
It is finished!	John 19:30
Father, into your hands…	Luke 23:46

- Create an experiential celebration for all ages by using "Way of the Cross" (see Appendix 4).
- Portray the story with different members of the congregation telling part of the story as one of the disciples. You may choose to have the characters dress in costumes; however, it will be more effective if the characters simply rise from among the congregation, dressed in their usual clothing, symbolizing that we all are disciples of Christ (see Appendix 5).
- In a simple service, act out the Last Supper (with only narration, no dramatics). Have the communion servers seated around a large table up front, At the appropriate time they receive the elements and then rise to take them to the congregation. Use Matthew 26:17–30 and 1 Corinthians 11:23–26. At the close, sing a hymn and leave as the disciples did.

Teaching Holy Week

- Make badges saying "Ask me about Holy Week" for persons who have learned the meaning of the special days. These will be worn during this special week.
- Create bulletin boards depicting the season. Use ashes for Ash Wednesday, palms and/or donkey for Palm Sunday, bread and cup for Maundy Thursday, the cross and crown of thorns for Good Friday, and butterflies, spring flowers, and empty tomb for Easter.
- Using a long strip of paper, make a time line of the events of Holy Week. Look up the following scripture for this: Matthew 21:12–13; Matthew 26:6–7; Luke 19:28–40; Luke 19:41–44; Luke 22:14–23; Mark 14:32–42; Matthew 26:47–56; Matthew 26:57–64; 27:11–31; Matthew 27:32–55; and Matthew 28:1–10.
- Color eggs and remember that they symbolize new life. Older children and adults may want to experiment with the Ukrainian tradition of drawing designs and symbols on the eggs with melted wax and dying them. (The part with wax will not take the color.) As you do this you can learn more about the symbols.
- Using the suggestions in "Nails in a cross" under "Celebrating Holy Week" (page 55), create discussion opportunities for a class.
- List "feeling" words that describe what happened to Jesus during the last week of his life. Then talk in groups of three about what your feelings are about Christianity. Is yours a "Good Friday" or an "Easter Morning" type of faith?
- Create an experiential learning for all ages by using "Way of the Cross" (see Appendix 4).
- Portray the story with different people telling part of the story as one of the disciples (see Appendix 5).

—9—

EASTER SUNDAY AND THE EASTER SEASON

The Easter Season begins on Easter Sunday and extends to Pentecost. Perhaps we should develop the habit of using the word "Sunday" to designate the difference between the Easter season and Easter Sunday. This would help us to remember that this occasion of Christ's resurrection is too important to limit the celebration to one day. It needs the whole fifty days to celebrate properly.

As Christians we begin our celebration of the resurrection of Christ on Easter; however, we actually borrowed the season and the name from pre-Christian days. People have always adapted symbols from surrounding religions and made them their own. Many of the Old Testament practices were adaptations of preexisting counterparts in the Canaanite religion, such as animal sacrifice, temple worship, circumcision, priests, and prophets. Passover may have been adapted from two Canaanite festivals, the spring birthing of livestock and celebration of the early barley harvest.

Christianity is no exception. The name "Easter" has an uncertain origin. Many believe it comes from the Anglo-Saxon goddess of renewal of life in spring, Eostre or Eastre. Since Christ's resurrection signifies our renewal of life, it would not be surprising for us to adopt the name and celebration for our purposes.

Many symbols of Easter have been adapted from various cultures. Even our cross is an instrument of death transformed into a symbol of new life. The sign of the fish is the unique and probably the earliest Christian symbol. The important thing here is not so much their origins but how these traditions and symbols have been transformed into true meaning in the Christian faith.

We can date the resurrection to the spring, because it followed the celebration of Passover in the spring. Passover may fall on different days of the week. The early Jewish Christians celebrated the day of the resurrection on the third day after Passover regardless of the day of the week, but the Gentile Christians insisted that it be celebrated on Sunday. In 325 C.E. the Council of Nicea set the date of celebration as the first Sunday after the full moon crosses the spring equinox. That date may vary by as many as thirty-five days, and so sometimes Easter comes in March and sometimes in April. Some Christians in other parts of the world use different dates.

Age-level Understandings

We must remember that young children cannot grasp abstract concepts. They do not yet have the experience of the concrete on which to base the abstract. So we concentrate on Easter as a special time when we remember Jesus. With any telling of the stories that include the death of Christ, we must be sure to follow up immediately (almost in the same breath) with a statement that God wouldn't let Jesus stay dead, and he was raised from the dead.

The symbols of new life, such as the egg and the bunny, can be enjoyed by children even though they do not understand the abstract connection with the resurrection. The egg symbolizes something that appears to be dead but has new life in it. The bunny spends most of the winter in a hole in the ground or some other protected place and comes out in spring, similar to how Jesus came back to life from the grave. New life is the heart of our Easter celebration—Christ's new life, and our new life because of him and because he died rather than compromise God's will for his life. And so these symbols of new life can be enjoyed by children, and they will later connect the abstract concept.

For additional suggestions for ways to introduce God, Jesus, the Bible, prayer, and the church to children and youth, see *How Do Our Children Grow?* by Delia Halverson (St. Louis: Chalice Press, 1999).

Celebrating the Easter Season

- Create visual imagery for worship using a reproduction of a grave in a cave by stacking several rocks to form an enclosure with one stone to the side as the stone rolled away. Inside the "cave," place a lighted candle to represent Christ coming from the tomb.
- Our Easter sunrise service comes from the tradition of Easter vigil. The vigil can begin any time after sundown on Saturday but is usually celebrated just before dawn on Easter Sunday. This service begins in darkness (reflecting the darkness at the close of the Good Friday service), and one candle is lit. From it other candles are lit by individual worshipers in the service, symbolizing the "new fire" of Christ in a dark world. Lights may then be turned on either all at once or in stages as the gospel is read.
- We wear new clothes on Easter to symbolize the new life we find in Christ. In the early church when the new converts were baptized at Easter, they then changed into new white clothes to symbolize new life in Christ.
- Celebrate Easter Sunday by renewing the vows taken at baptism, remembering how you are renewed by Christ.

- The colors associated with the Easter season are white and gold. White signifies the purity and newness of victory over sin and death, and the gold (or yellow) symbolizes the risen Christ who came to enlighten the world. Gold also symbolizes Christ as king.
- On Easter Sunday release butterflies. You may order the caterpillars early and watch them as they become butterflies. Check out the web sites: *www.insectlore.com; www.butterflywebsite.com* (Note: This may not be appropriate if Easter Sunday is early and you live in very cold climate.)
- Invite worshipers to bring flowers from their gardens to create a live cross. Use a cross that has been a part of your Lenten experience and wrap it with chicken wire. As worshipers arrive they will add their flowers to the cross, creating a colorful reminder of new life. This may be done in the sanctuary or outside the door. Place it on the church lawn for all to see during the next few days. Remove it once the flowers wilt. (Note: If garden flowers are not available, ask a florist to save the unused flowers from the past few days for you.)
- Plan an Easter sunrise service. There are many suggestions available. Be sure that it is more than a "routine" service. It might include drama, dramatic readings, communion, interpretive dance, and certainly music. If the weather is conducive, have it outdoors, but pay attention to the location. I've attended sunrise services in every location, from a mountainside to seashore to churchyards. On the mountainside we simply held hands in a circle, greeting the sunrise with song and prayers. By the seaside I was with a large crowd at a park, but the preacher and music were on a truck-bed beside a Dumpster, not very conducive to worship. One service I attended was in the churchyard, but our backs were to the rising sun, and all we saw in front of us were a building and a portable piano. The next year we turned the worshipers around so that we could enjoy the sunrise, and we added drama to the worship.

- For a sunrise service, sing "America the Beautiful" and remember that it was written by Katharine Lee Bates in 1893 after viewing the sunrise from Pike's Peak.
- As you begin the Easter service, have everyone gather outside and keep the sanctuary dark. Give worshipers candles to light and/or flowers to carry, and enter the building remembering how the women rose at dawn to go to the tomb and found it empty. When everyone is inside, flood the room with light and celebrate.
- Have a worship with "lessons and carols," alternating scripture with Easter hymns.
- On Easter Sunday create a cross with Easter lilies or other potted flowers. This may be done with stands of varying heights, or it may be done by making a cross from 6" boards with holes in the boards to hold the flower pots. Prop the cross slightly to keep the pots from falling out.
- Use a strolling actor to tell the story. The actor comes down the aisle, greeting people and saying that he or she recalls the story and then begins to tell it. The story is then told from the viewpoint of some character in the story, such as a disciple or one of the women who went to the tomb.
- Greet each other with the phrase "Alleluia, the Lord is risen!" Originally the word "Alleluia" was used only at Easter.

Teaching the Easter Season

- Make badges saying "Ask me about the Easter Season" for persons who have learned the meaning of the season. These will be worn during this special season.
- Create bulletin boards and leave them up throughout Easter Season. Use butterflies, spring flowers, and other new things of spring, and the empty tomb.
- If you made a time line of the events leading up to Easter (see page 57), add those that happened after Easter Sunday to this. Realize that since these events are reported in different gospels, we cannot be certain about their order. Look up the following scriptures: John 20:19–23; Matthew 28:11–15;

John 20:26–31; Luke 24:13–35; Matthew 28:16–20; Luke 24:36–49; John 21:1–25; Luke 24:50–53.

- Study the resurrection story in all four gospels and note how the different writers have told the story differently.
- Ask students to recall a time when they didn't think they had a chance for something that did come through. This may have been the way that Jesus' disciples felt after the crucifixion, but Easter morning brought a second opportunity for new life.
- On Easter Sunday ask the Sunday school classes to create posters telling the news of Jesus' resurrection. Post these around the church, changing them periodically during the Easter Season.
- Using four columns and working with the four gospels, write the events of Easter morning so that you can tell which events are recorded by multiple gospels and how they differ. The book *Gospel Parallels* will help with this.
- Approach the story of Thomas' doubting with recognition that to question was a part of Thomas' faith journey. Inquiring into our beliefs is a path of faith development that we all must journey if we are to really mature in our faith. If we do not inquire, then the belief is not truly ours, but a belief we've only borrowed.

—10—

PENTECOST SUNDAY

Pentecost is sometimes called the birthday of the church because it was the time when the followers of Christ really bonded together into a body, ignited with the Holy Spirit and prepared to spread the Word. The story comes from Acts 2:1–42. The Hebrew celebration of Pentecost came at the close of their early harvest. (Remember that this was a subtropical climate and harvest came early.) People from many countries were in Jerusalem for the celebration. In the midst of the disciples' searching for direction, the Holy Spirit came to their aid, just as Jesus had promised.

Immediately following this, Peter urged people to repent and be baptized. This was the start of the tradition to baptize persons at Pentecost, and some churches use this day for confirmation today. In some places, particularly England, Pentecost goes by the name of Whitsunday or White Sunday because of the practice of baptizing new members on this day. In the early church new members wore white robes when they were baptized, and today some churches carry on the tradition of wearing white for baptism.

The Hebrew celebration of what we now call Pentecost had several names. It was called the Day of First Fruits, Festival of Weeks, and Shabuoth. The biblical reference to this festival is found in Leviticus 23:15–16. By Jesus' day the celebration had lost much of its agricultural flavor and was associated with God's creation of the people and their religious history. In this celebration they emphasized the occasion on Mount Sinai (where the temple sat) when God gave the gift of the *Torah* (the Law). The Greeks gave the day a different name, using their word for five, *penta*, or *pentekoste hmera*, meaning the fiftieth day.

Like Easter, the day of Pentecost is determined by the cycle of the moon, and so it changes every year. It is set for fifty days (the seventh Sunday) after Easter. It may occur any time between May 10 and June 13. This celebration may be forgotten on the years that it happens on Mother's Day or Memorial Day weekend. But it is too important an occasion for us to push aside.

The color we use for Pentecost is red, which is also considered the color symbolic of the church. This represents the tongues of fire that are reported to have been on the heads of those present. The theme is a celebration of hope and renewal of purpose and mission.

Age-level Understandings

Pentecost can be celebrated in a way that children will really enjoy. They love festive celebrations and birthday parties. However, because they usually only understand the church as their own congregation and their understanding of time and history is limited, they may not grasp the great heritage that Pentecost brings.

For additional suggestions for ways to introduce God, Jesus, the Bible, prayer, and the church to children and youth, see *How Do Our Children Grow?* by Delia Halverson (St. Louis: Chalice Press, 1999).

Celebrating Pentecost

- Create visual imagery in worship using: flames; kites (representing breath/wind); rocks (symbolizing the church's foundation); red peppers (representing how we are "on fire for Christ"); birthday cake for the church (asking each person to make a "wish" for the church and blow out candles).

- Use audio imagery by having wind chimes that will be rung at specific times. Use wind instruments for special music and mention the symbolism of wind and the coming of the Holy Spirit. Play a tape of wind sounds during the service.

- Use red (the color for Pentecost) in every way possible on this day: red paraments and vestments; red floral arrangement; red ink in the bulletin; a red bulletin cover; red and white candles; red balloons; red paper covering doors; red banners indoors and in parking lot; red ribbons on pew ends; red crepe paper streamers; red confetti (arrange for cleanup).

- Use visual imagery in a processional by inviting children to carry sticks with red streamers, red balloons, embroidery hoops with red streamers.

- Encourage people to wear red clothing for this day. Recognize the red colors in the service.

- Create a litany for the occasion and give worshipers a red ribbon to wave at appropriate times.

- Celebrate by using hymns of unity and hymns that indicate the coming of the Holy Spirit, such as:

  "Blest Be the Tie That Binds"
  "I'm Goin' a Sing When the Spirit Says Sing"
  "Kum Ba Yah"
  "See How Great a Flame Aspires"
  "Spirit of the Living God"
  "Surely the Presence of the Lord Is in This Place"
  "We Are the Church"

- At Pentecost there were people from many countries, speaking different languages. During the greeting time of the service, invite persons to greet those around them in different languages. The words for the greeting can be printed in the bulletin in different languages.

- Read scripture in different languages, remembering how everyone heard the word in their own languages on Pentecost.
- During the scripture reading, have the leader read Acts 2:1–4 and then three or four people (who have been asked to do this ahead of time) stand and read verse 4 again in other languages. Then the leader reads verses 5–21.
- Pray the Lord's Prayer in different languages at the same time.
- During a time of "Passing the Peace," invite persons to share with a neighbor some way in which the Holy Spirit is working in their lives.
- Give each person a red flower or ribbon to wear.
- Spread a red "carpet" or red streamers down the aisles of the sanctuary.
- Use liturgical dance with dancers dressed in red with red streamers.
- Use a strolling actor to tell the story. The actor comes down the aisle, greeting people and saying that he or she recalls the story and then begins to tell it. The story is then told from the viewpoint of someone who was in the house when the Holy Spirit came.
- Lead a guided meditation, asking the worshipers to imagine that they are actually at Pentecost. At points in the meditation, ask them to think about what they would be seeing, hearing, or feeling at that moment. Close by singing "Spirit of the Living God, Fall Afresh on Me."
- Place a tree in the sanctuary and decorate it with symbols or words illustrating the fruits of the Spirit from Galatians 5:22–23.
- Celebrate new beginnings:

    Celebrate new gifts of ministry in your church—ministries you have been able to do in the past year that you never did before.

    Celebrate new members in the past year, recognizing them and what they contribute to your church.

Celebrate walls or barriers that have broken down during the past year, in your church, in your community, and in the world.

Celebrate friendships or relationships that have been renewed or mended.

- Make footprints from red construction paper and place them on the sidewalk and in the hallways leading into the sanctuary, inviting people to your festive celebration.
- The dove is a symbol of the Holy Spirit. Make origami doves (or doves cut from flat poster board) and give one to each worshiper.
- Have someone dressed in biblical costume come into the sanctuary and tell the worshipers about Pentecost as if he or she had just experienced it.
- Use a quiet time or centering time during the service, asking worshipers to listen for the coming of the Holy Spirit in their lives.
- Ask worshipers to contribute to your worship setting by bringing a red flowering plant. These will be placed in the worship center and then planted on the grounds afterwards, declaring to the world that you are "on fire" for Christ.
- Use windsocks or embroidery hoops with red and white ribbons in the sanctuary, remembering how the Holy Spirit came as a rush of wind at Pentecost.
- Preach on the gifts we can offer to God, and pass out flame shapes cut from construction paper. Ask each person to write on the flame a gift he or she can give to God and place it on the altar table, or pass baskets to gather the flames and place them together on the altar table.
- Honor persons who have had significant leadership in the early formation of your own church.
- See "Barriers broken down" on page 10.
- See "Stump from a tree" on page 10.
- As people leave the service, give each a red candle or a candle with a red bow to use at home, remembering how the Holy Spirit comes into our lives.

- Pentecost is sometimes called the birthday of the church. Have a birthday party, but don't stop by emphasizing the past. Celebrate the present and future acts of the church. Place a candle on the cake and light it for each ministry or mission that you do in your church, and then place unlit candles for those that you anticipate doing in the future.
- Create an all-church banner. Make a large banner of white fabric. At the top place a descending dove, outlined in red. Place the banner on a large table at the entrance to the sanctuary. Beside the banner place many types of red fabrics (various shades and prints), glue, scissors, and several patterns for various sizes and shapes of flames. Invite each person to cut out a flame, or several flames, and place them from the bottom of the banner, ascending toward the dove. They may put their names on the flames. Bring the banner to the front while singing, "We Are the Church."
- Include communion in your Pentecost celebration and invite several families to bake different breads from other cultures. Use this bread for communion. Have those who baked the bread bring it forward in a procession and present it at the altar. Each bread may be wrapped in a fabric typical of that country.
- Worship with another faith or culture and then enjoy a picnic together afterwards. Make pinwheels and fly kites, remembering that the Holy Spirit came on those early Christians as a gushing wind.

Teaching Pentecost

- Make badges saying "Ask me about Pentecost" for persons who have learned the meaning of the season. These will be worn during this special day.
- Create a bulletin board with a display of the history of the church, locally, nationally, and internationally.
- At Pentecost the people not only had a language barrier but also a communication barrier involving customs, culture, and traditions. Think of terms we understand that someone from

another culture would not understand, even if they knew English (e.g., "high five," "eat up," "cool," and many terms used in sports).

- Compare the Tower of Babel (Gen. 11:1–9) with Pentecost (Acts 2:1–21). The Tower of Babel produced mass confusion, and Pentecost produced unity.
- Pentecost actually stresses oneness or unity with diversity— not conformity, but unity. Discuss the difference between conformity and unity.
- Make mobiles with Pentecost symbols and display them around the church.
- Make wall hangings or posters with symbols of the past, present, and future of the church.
- Draw a large body on paper and have everyone write or draw pictures of how the church helps others. Title the poster, "The hands of Christ in the world today."
- Take red flowers to shut-ins, explaining the symbolism.
- Write prayers on kites and then fly them.
- Visit the sanctuary and look for symbols of the Holy Spirit.
- Ask a longtime member of the local church to visit the classroom and tell how that particular church got started. Then follow it up with a discussion of what the "universal church" means.
- Ask persons who have been members of various churches, both of your denomination and others, speak of the commonality they see between the churches they've belonged to.
- Experience a Pentecost by darkening the room and sitting in a circle with a burning candle in a large metal bowl placed in the middle. Read Acts 2:1–4a. Ask each person to write on a card some worry, mistake, suffering, pain, rejection, or disappointment. Then ask them to throw these into the Pentecostal fire. Symbolically, from the flame, these problems are purified, and we rise to new life and forgiveness.
- Make paper chains, writing the fruits of the Spirit (Galatians 5:22–23) on each link.

- Use red tempera paint to place handprints on a banner.
- Bring a deflated beach ball into the classroom. Ask class members to bounce the ball. Blow up the ball and then bounce it. Talk about how we too must be filled by the Holy Spirit in order to do what we are made to do.
- Make birth announcements for the church.
- Write a newspaper article about the happenings at Pentecost.
- Talk about ways that the Holy Spirit works in people's lives and make ribbon banners with words such as *empowers, leads, guides, directs, inspires, urges, heartens.*
- Plan an evening time when you can tell the Pentecost story around a bonfire or in front of a fireplace. If you use a bonfire, be sure to check on local regulations.
- To recognize how the Holy Spirit is at work in each of us, create a "You're Special Tree." Make hearts of paper with a hole in them to string on the tree. Each person has one heart for every other person in the class. They will write something that makes each person special, placing the name on the heart along with the "specialness" of that person. These are hung on the tree and at the end of the session given to the person to take home.

—11—

ORDINARY TIME OR THE SEASON AFTER PENTECOST

Use of the word "Ordinary" for this time frame does not mean mundane or common, but rather comes from the word "ordinal" which means, simply, counted or chronological time, the time in order. It begins on the Sunday after Pentecost (or Trinity Sunday) and ends the last Sunday before the beginning of Advent (or Christ the King Sunday).

It is only appropriate that the season after Pentecost places an emphasis on spreading the gospel throughout the world, since the Holy Spirit brought communication skills to the disciples at Pentecost. At this time, as we remember our mission to carry the message beyond Pentecost and into the world, we must come down from the "mountaintop" and live in the real world with our Christianity. This is a time for exploring peace, forgiveness, and building community, not only in our churches and towns, but around the world. This is also a time when we explore creation and what it means to be created by God and to be cocreators with God.

Some churches break up this time into two sections, calling the first Pentecost Season (lasting until the next to last Sunday of August) and the second Kingdomtide or Dominiontide (the last Sunday in August until Advent). Kingdomtide is the time when we work to build up the kingdom.

Age-level Understandings

Children have a natural curiosity about people in other countries. They will not hold prejudice unless we teach it to them with our actions as well as words. This is a good time to take inventory of your equipment and materials in the nurseries and classrooms. Do they encourage diversity, or are all of the toys typical of your own race and culture? Are the pictures of Jesus in the materials and curriculum expressive of his ethnic background? What do bulletin boards and posters around the church say about cultural diversity?

Take a look at your curriculum and methods of teaching. Is it a "tourist" approach, where children only see people as strange, wearing different clothes, eating different food, and distanced from us? Unless children learn about their own background as one of many cultures, and unless your teaching incorporates many cultures at *all* times, this becomes "shotgun education." Instead of studying one culture at a time, it is better to study different areas of life from many cultures at once, such as how people farm in several cultures, not saying one is better than another, but that they are simply different. Children will enjoy:

- Using play items of different races and cultures
- Learning words for names and numbers in other languages
- Singing songs, telling stories, and playing games of different cultures
- Learning about their own ethnic background
- Learning about heroes of their own ethnic background and others'

Foundations can be formed with young children that will help them in the future as they make and maintain relationships with various ethnic groups. Build experiences into your teaching that enable children to:

- Enjoy a trusting environment as a foundation of future understanding
- Build appreciation of themselves as a foundation for understanding care for others
- Learn about similarities and differences
- Develop group skills that lead to a sense of belonging and love for another
- Appreciate their own talents and abilities
- Accept responsibility for their own actions and learn how their actions affect others
- Grow with praise for their positive actions
- Know persons of different cultures who have positive attitudes

Children learn best by experience, and so we want them to learn through the experiences in our classrooms that Christ came for all peoples and that the message that Christ brought us was spread around the world after Pentecost.

For additional suggestions for ways to introduce God, Jesus, the Bible, prayer, and the church to children and youth, see *How Do Our Children Grow?* by Delia Halverson (St. Louis: Chalice Press, 1999).

Celebrating the Season after Pentecost or Ordinary Time

- Create visual imagery in worship using: live potter molding a pot or various pots (symbolizing how we are vessels to carry out God's message); oxen yoke (symbolizing how we can accomplish God's work when yoked with Christ); items from other cultures that symbolize the many facets of God.
- Sing hymns such as:

    "Christ for the World We Sing"
    "Here I Am, Lord"
    "In Christ There Is No East or West"
    "Pass It On"
    "We've a Story to Tell to the Nations"

Teaching the Season after Pentecost or Ordinary Time

- Create bulletin boards with pictures of Christians in other countries or missionaries who are carrying the message to people elsewhere. You can also create a bulletin board showing how we share the message of Christ in our own community.
- Clip pictures and stories that depict people suffering. Ask how we can relieve the suffering of others.
- Celebrate our growth in our understanding of God. In Genesis 11:1–9 the people understood that God caused the confusion and set barriers between the people. In Acts 2:1–21 we recognize that God actually creates unity in a positive way and breaks down barriers. Notice that the Genesis reference does not actually say they were evil. Is that our interpretation?
- The season after Pentecost is a good time to stress the covenant we make when we join the church. Review your membership vows, and create opportunities for stressing those vows. If your membership vows pledge your prayers, presence, gifts, and service, each week provide a table at the entrance of the classroom with a place to:

    1. List prayer concerns   Prayers

    2. Register attendance   Presence

    3. Leave an offering   Gifts

    4. List something they have   Service
       done this week for
       someone else

- Create "Story Circles" of four to six people. Remind the class that during this season we concentrate on sharing our faith with others. Each person will share the following stories:

    God's story   Share your favorite Bible story.

    My story   Tell of someone who has
                         influenced your Christian
                         faith.

Our story   Tell of a time when you have
                                      influenced another.

- Place a large picture of Christ in the center of the bulletin
  board. Have pictures of the church in action (missions,
  worshiping, etc.), and have each student select a picture and
  place it in a circle around Christ's picture, telling about what
  is happening in the picture. Then place the following label
  on the poster: "We are Christ's hands today." An alternative
  to using pictures is to draw around students' hands, write a
  positive act or a mission that the church does on the hands,
  and then place the hands around the picture.

—12—

OTHER SPECIAL DAYS

—TRINITY SUNDAY—

Trinity Sunday is celebrated on the Sunday after Pentecost. Because Pentecost falls during the week, we often celebrate Pentecost on the following Sunday, and Trinity Sunday gets lost in the shuffle. Young children have difficulty with the abstract concept of the Trinity (see "Age-level Understandings" below), and consequently it is seldom featured in children's curriculum.

Indeed, many adults struggle with the Trinity, because at first glance it appears that we are dividing God into three separate deities to worship. It sometimes helps to recognize that through the Trinity we have three different ways of understanding God: God as creator and sustainer, God in a human experience (God with "skin on"), and God who works within us.

Age-level Understandings

Over the years people have tried to find ways to explain the Trinity to children. I have heard everything from an egg to a triangle. These are all good abstract concepts, but we must recognize that children do not think in abstract terms. They can easily repeat definitions that we may give them, but the best we can do within their understanding is to say that using symbols of three reminds us of God, Jesus, and the Holy Spirit. Their grasp of the Trinity will come later. Just as we do not teach algebra (which is abstract in understanding) before simple addition (which is concrete), we do not try to teach all theological concepts to children at once.

For additional suggestions for ways to introduce God, Jesus, the Bible, prayer, and the church to children and youth, see *How Do Our Children Grow?* by Delia Halverson (St. Louis: Chalice Press, 1999).

Celebrating Trinity Sunday

- Use several creeds during the service, comparing them for their statements of belief.
- Create a bulletin cover using various Trinitarian symbols, such as the trefoil, three intertwined circles, fleur-de-lis, shamrock, or triangle.
- The Trinity expresses God in three ways. Experiment with various images of God and various ways to praise God.
- Use creeds in worship that Sunday school classes have created.
- Invite the congregation to spontaneously express their beliefs in a creed. To do this, print the following in the bulletin. Ahead of time ask two people for each of the three sections to be prepared to offer a word or phrase in their respective areas.

> We believe that God comes to us in many ways.
>
> We believe that God created these things: *(During this time, feel free to mention out loud things that you recognize as created by God.)*
>
> We believe that God came in human form, and through Jesus taught us these things: *(During this time, feel free to mention out loud various truths that Jesus taught.)*
>
> We believe that God works within us as the Holy Spirit: *(During this time, feel free to mention out loud ways that the Holy Spirit helps us live better lives.)*

- Use hymns that express different images of God, such as:

  "Come, Thou Almighty King"
  "God Hath Spoken by the Prophets"
  "God of Many Names"
  "God of the Sparrow"
  "How Like a Gentle Spirit"
  "Maker, in Whom We Live"
  "Many Gifts, One Spirit"
  "On Eagle's Wings"
  "Our Parent, by Whose Name"

Teaching Trinity Sunday

- Youth and adults can study some of the historic creeds of the church. Then ask the students to create a creed reflecting their own beliefs, using their everyday language.
- Using the beginning phrase "God is like…," ask for suggestions of ways we can understand what God is like.
- Give each person a large piece of paper and markers and ask them to draw symbols or pictures that remind them of the Trinity, putting one in each corner of the triangle.
- Use various symbols for the Trinity to create a collage of symbols.

—WORLDWIDE COMMUNION—

This celebratory Sunday is fairly recent in origin. It was established so that all Christians everywhere might receive communion on the same date. It has a uniting factor, and builds community across the time zones and around the world.

This is a time to recognize our common love for Christ, no matter what our particular denomination or nationality.

Age-level Understandings

The abstract concepts of communion are outside most children's concrete understanding; in fact, many adults cannot understand communion. It is important for children to understand communion as a time when we gather as a church family to remember Jesus in a special way. Children can recognize Worldwide Communion Sunday as a time when Christians all over the world have the meal that reminds us of how Jesus ate the last meal with his disciples. The vastness of the world is beyond the grasp of young children, and you may need to concentrate on other churches in your community for them, instead of churches worldwide.

For additional suggestions on communion and for ways to introduce God, Jesus, the Bible, prayer, and the church to children and youth, see *How Do Our Children Grow?* by Delia Halverson (St. Louis: Chalice Press, 1999).

Celebrating Worldwide Communion

- Create visual imagery in worship using: globe, dove (symbolizing peace), objects from many nations/cultures.
- Have members of the congregation bake bread from various countries and use these for communion. Invite those who baked the bread to bring it forward during the singing of a hymn. The bread may be wrapped in a fabric typical of the country.
- Print greetings in different languages in the bulletin. Have a time in the service when each person chooses a language and greets someone near them in that language.
- Use hymns such as:

> "Blest Be the Tie That Binds"
> "Christ for the World We Sing"
> "For the Healing of the Nations"
> "God of Grace and God of Glory"
> "Help Us Accept Each Other"
> "Let There Be Light"
> "Let There Be Peace on Earth"
> "Lift Every Voice and Sing"
> "O God of Every Nation"
> "Shalom to You"

"There's a Spirit in the Air"
"There's a Wideness in God's Mercy"
"This Is a Day of New Beginning"
"Your Love, O God, Is Broad"

Teaching Worldwide Communion

- Make badges saying "Ask me about Worldwide Communion Sunday" for persons who have learned the meaning of the day. These will be worn during this special day.
- Each year center your learning on one particular country or area of the world. Learn about the people there, their customs in celebrating communion, and something about your church's influence in that country. If you have had mission teams working in the country, learn about their experiences. Bake a bread that is typical of that country and ask that it be used for your communion service.
- As a class, write a letter to a class in another country asking them about their traditions in the church and sharing some of the things that your class likes best about your own church.
- See the section "Age-level Understandings" in chapter 11 for ideas of ways to teach a broader understanding of all people everywhere.

—ALL SAINTS' DAY/HALLOWEEN—

Before Christ, the Celts celebrated the end of the summer and prepared for the coming of the dark months the only way they knew how. This celebration was on October 31. Since their religion believed that evil spirits hovered over the Earth, ready to pounce on them in the dark, they burned fires and made animal sacrifices to keep the evil spirits away. They did not have the scientific knowledge that we have today, and so they believed that witches had magical powers. The word "witch" comes from the Anglo-Saxon word *wicce*, or "wise one," and it was originally thought that they possessed magic for both good and evil. Witches were believed to cause storms, diseases, and deaths. A woman could be declared a witch simply because she had a birthmark or because she had an ability to float in water. Anything that the people could not understand was blamed on evil spirits and witches. Today, instead of relying on superstition, we understand many scientific laws of our world and can predict natural disasters. We know that many diseases come about through germs and lack of sanitation. We can warn people who are likely to have heart attacks, and our scientists are working to discover causes for cancer and other illnesses that cause untimely deaths.

While the Celts were practicing their religion, Christianity was growing in the Roman Empire. As Christianity began to span over generations, there were more and more people who had died for their beliefs and who were remembered in special ways. The Roman church set aside special days to remember specific persons, designating them as "saints." When it became evident that there were more "saints" than days to celebrate, the church established a specific day to commemorate all those who did not have a special day set aside for them.

In the ninth century, to combat the old Celtic religion in the British Isles, the church proclaimed November 1 as All Saints' Day and the night of October 31 as All Hallows' Eve, or Halloween. Christianity brought the bright side of the holiday, switching the emphasis from worship of evil to the worship of the true God. This combination points out the difference that Christianity made in the world.

Today we recognize each person as a "saint," whether living or dead, and so All Saints' Day is now broader than the celebration of those who have died. We celebrate all who love the Lord as saints. We see this time as an occasion to remember our heritage, those who have gone before us, and also an opportunity to recognize our responsibility to carry Christianity forward as the living saints of today.

Hebrews 12:1–2 and 2 Timothy 1:2–5 are good scriptures that affirm our celebration of the saints of today and of the past.

Age-level Understandings

Although children cannot grasp the span of centuries that encompasses all those who are a part of our faith heritage, they can appreciate adults in their lives who show them Christ. We can also introduce them to various people, both dead and living, who have made a difference in our world. Children typically find adults and youth that they will model their lives after. Without these people that they can use as models, they will have difficulty growing spiritually.

For additional suggestions for ways to introduce God, Jesus, the Bible, prayer, and the church to children and youth, see *How Do Our Children Grow?* by Delia Halverson (St. Louis: Chalice Press, 1999).

Celebrating All Saints' Day

- Create visual imagery in worship using: bright and dark objects; unique roots (symbolizing the saints of the past as the roots of our heritage); woven cloth (symbolizing how the saints of the past and today weave the fabric of our faith); vocational symbols (symbolizing how we carry our vocation as a "saint" into our career lives—be certain to include symbols from school to help children and youth recognize that they have an opportunity to be living "saints" at school).
- Give each person a name tag that they fill in: _____, A Saint of God.
- Use banners with symbols of saints of the past. These may be on standards and used in a processional or simply displayed around the sanctuary.
- Assign a specific period of church history to each Sunday school class and ask them to research a saint during that era and give a two-sentence statement about the saint during worship.
- See "Stump from a tree" on page 10.
- Place colorful streamers on standards near the entrance. On a table beside the streamers place baskets of small bells. Ask each worshiper to select a bell and pin it on the streamers in

memory or in honor of someone who has made a difference in their spiritual growth. At the opening of the service, bring the standard of streamers forward, swaying the standard to make the bells ring.
- Use hymns and songs such as:

> "I Sing a Song of the Saints of God"
> "When the Saints Go Marching In"
> "For All the Saints"
> "They'll Know We Are Christians by Our Love"

Teaching All Saints' Day/Halloween

- Create a bulletin board display of "saints" of the past and "saints" of today. Include a mirror in the section of "Saints of Today."
- Create a bulletin board of light and dark, labeling the dark "Without Christ" and the light "With Christ." Title the board "Halloween/All Saints' Day."
- Create a litany of thanksgiving for all saints, living and dead.
- Research the word *saint* as it is used in the Old and New Testaments.
- Learn from other Christian groups about their traditions (prayers, songs, and symbols) for All Saints' Day.
- Have persons dress as saints of the past and visit classrooms telling their stories.
- Make badges saying "Ask me about All Saints' Day" for persons who have learned the meaning of the day. These will be worn during this special day.
- Several weeks before All Saints' Day, interview each member of the class and write up a brief biography of each and why they love God. Put these in a booklet to be handed out on All Saints' Day. Title the booklet "Saints of Today".

—Thanksgiving—

In the United States, the roots of our Thanksgiving celebration go back to the time when the early settlers struggled through hardship (almost half of the settlers had died) but still found they had thankful hearts. Although this is not specifically a religious holiday, we can take this opportunity to live out our special thanks. The Hebrew heritage of a thanksgiving celebration was called the Feast of Tabernacles or Booths. They created a *sukkah* for this. You can read more about it under "Celebrating Thanksgiving" below.

Even more important than counting the things we have to be thankful for, such an occasion should turn our eyes toward others who are less fortunate and help us to see ways that we can help them as Jesus would have done.

Age-level Understandings

Children can name many material things that they are thankful for, but it is important that they recognize that the significant things in our lives are not the material items, but other people and our opportunity to help them. If we center our thoughts on "thanksliving" instead of "thanksgiving," then we will give thanks but also live out our thanks.

For additional suggestions for ways to introduce God, Jesus, the Bible, prayer, and the church to children and youth, see *How Do Our Children Grow?* by Delia Halverson (St. Louis: Chalice Press, 1999).

Celebrating Thanksgiving

- Create visual imagery in worship using: fruits of the earth; pictures or sculptures of people; symbols of learning institutions; items from nature, such as a glass of water; or use expressions from your own setting or community (farming—seed, fruits, earth; manufacturing—products that meet human needs).
- Gather outside the sanctuary before the service and give families symbols of things for which we are thankful (or ask each person to bring such a symbol or to bring some food item to share with a soup kitchen). As you enter singing a processional song, each person brings his or her symbol or gift forward to the altar area.

- Have each person write down or draw something that he or she can offer of self to someone else. These become a part of the offering.
- Before the service, invite families/people to write down or talk in their families about special gifts, blessings, or surprises they have experienced during the last year. (You might ask people to share these with those sitting near them during your welcoming time.) Have the people offer these during the Thanksgiving worship by naming them verbally during a special time or writing them down and placing them in the offering plate or on the altar table.
- Use the story of Ruth, which is believed to have been read at the Jewish Feast of Weeks, a celebration of thanks.
- Create a *sukkah* (a booth or open shed with three walls used during the Hebrew harvest as shelter) by lashing poles together and covering the top with branches. Fruits and vegetables are hung from the overhead poles. The biblical reference to this is Leviticus 23:40. Later the *sukkah* came to represent the "temporariness" of life on Earth. It became an eight-day festival of prayer, feasting, and rejoicing. The booth should not be saved from year to year because it is a "temporary" symbol.
- Use wheat at the entrances to the sanctuary, indicating your thanks for the harvest.
- Involve people of other cultures, inviting them to dress in a native costume and share something about their thanksgiving celebration.
- Use the story of the ten lepers and the one who returned to thank Jesus. This paints a broader view of Thanksgiving, beyond simply being thankful for food.

Teaching Thanksgiving

- Make badges saying "Ask me about Thanksgiving" for persons who have learned the meaning of the season. These will be worn during this special day.

- Create a bulletin board display of things for which we give thanks. You might make it interactive in several ways: make it three-dimensional so that foodstuffs may be added to the base of the bulletin board; put cut-out items of things we are thankful for in a basket beside the bulletin board and invite persons to place an item on the bulletin board; make an opportunity for persons to draw items of thanks on the bulletin board.
- Invite the whole church to bring vegetables on the Sunday before Thanksgiving. Begin boiling a big pot of beef or chicken stock on the stove. As vegetables are dropped off, clean them, cut them, and place them in the pot. At the close of worship invite everyone to enjoy a meal of soup and tell the story of Stone Soup. Be sure to emphasize the story as an opportunity to share and not as a trickery. If more food is brought than needed for the soup, or if you have any soup left over, take it to a soup kitchen.
- Help children recognize how our food is grown and processed with the many helpers of God. You might plan field trips to visit some of these helpers. Include God's helpers in your expressions of thankfulness.
- See "Create a *sukkah*" above. This may be done quickly by turning a table upside down and tying poles to the four legs for support. Tie onions and corn to the outside and to the poles. Lemons, gourds, pumpkins, baskets, and other items may be tied from and placed on the overhead supports. This is a symbol of harvest shared by both Jews and Christians.
- During a snack or meal time, place three kernels of corn beside each plate. Each person tells of three special times or events or persons from the past year that they are thankful for.

—APPENDIX 1—

SENTENCES FOR YOUR WORSHIP BULLETIN

These brief definitions may be used in bulletins or newsletters on a regular basis. Permission has been granted by the publisher of this book for you to do so. I'd suggest that you create a regular spot or separate box in which to place these so that the worshipers know each Sunday to go to that spot to learn a little more about worship and the symbols that we use in our churches. You might title these: "Do You Know about Worship?" The definitions have been arranged by subject so that you can choose what is appropriate for specific Sundays. There are also some general ones that may be used on Sundays that have no special significance. Not all definitions are appropriate for all churches, obviously.

Celebrating in worship and learning will also be enhanced when you can weave some of this information into the sermon or the actual worship service itself. For an example of this, see Appendix 3, "Hanging of the Greens."

Baptism
- The baptismal font remains in the chancel even when there is no baptism. We do this to remind us each Sunday of our baptism vows.
- Water, used in baptism, reminds us that God can remove our past sins; God refreshes us; God is the life-source without which we cannot live.
- There are three forms of baptism practiced in Protestant churches: sprinkling, pouring, immersion. Sprinkling reminds us that God's love showers down on us like the rain, giving us the spiritual nourishment that we need. Pouring reminds us that God's love is poured out on us. Immersion reminds

90

us that we are totally immersed in God's love and that love can cleanse us.

Benediction

• The benediction is not a prayer, but rather a "sending forth." It is appropriate to lift your head to receive this blessing and acknowledge being sent out to do Christ's work in the world.

Bible

• We use a large Bible on the altar or communion table to signify the importance of the Bible in our lives.
• Use of such words as *art* and *thy* come from the King James Version of the Bible. When this translation came into being, such terms were used only with good friends and family. Our pronouns *you* and *your* were reserved for royalty. This indicates that God is very personal to us.

Chancel

• The area at the front of the sanctuary, or the chancel, is raised, symbolizing that we lift God above all else in the world.
• The design of the front of some sanctuaries is called a divided chancel. This design places the altar or communion table as central; the pulpit, where the preacher delivers the message, on one side; and the lectern on the other side. This is where the liturgist and others assisting in the service stand.
• The design of the front of some sanctuaries is called pulpit-centered. This design does not have a lectern and puts primary emphasis on the message being spoken from the pulpit. This was common during the middle of the nineteenth and early twentieth centuries and is still used in some churches today.

Communion

• The communion elements symbolize our accepting Christ into our bodies. This acceptance is as essential to us as food and drink. We go forth as changed persons.
• There are several names we use for this meal of remembrance: eucharist, communion, Last Supper, Lord's supper.
• The bread or wafer of communion represents the body of

Christ, and the juice or wine represents the blood that Christ shed at his crucifixion.

- Wine was more common a drink than water in biblical times because the water was not purified. Some Protestant churches use grape juice instead of wine out of respect for persons with addiction problems.
- "Open communion" indicates that a church accepts anyone to participate who is anxious to follow Christ, no matter what his or her church affiliation.
- None of us fully understands what happens at communion. In many churches children are included so that they recognize that they are a part of the church family.
- The single chalice (cup or goblet) and loaf of bread symbolize the unity of Christians.
- In some churches the communion rail extends around the table where the elements are placed. This symbolizes a family meal, similar to the one that Jesus had with his disciples at their last supper.
- Some churches are designed with the communion table in the center of the sanctuary with the congregation seated around it. This creates a "family" atmosphere.
- The words "Do this in remembrance of me" are inscribed on the front of some communion tables or altars. This helps us remember that Christ instructed us to celebrate this meal of bread and cup together, as he did with his disciples.

Congregation

- The word *congregation* is derived from a verb meaning "to flock together." The word *church* comes from a New Testament word that we translate as "assembly." Therefore, the people, not the building, are the church. The building only offers a place for the true church to meet, giving us reminders of our vocation as Christians.

Creeds

- A creed is a list or statement of beliefs. Our church uses a variety of creeds throughout the year. The Apostles' Creed was written almost 2,000 years ago in order to identify the beliefs of the early church.

- In the Apostles' Creed the word *catholic* is not capitalized. This means the universal church, or the church that is all over the world, not just one denomination.

Hymns

- We stand for the opening hymn; this is similar to the custom of standing when a king enters the room. This recognizes Christ as our king.
- The first part of our service usually includes a hymn of adoration and praise. To grasp some understanding of adoration, imagine simply "looking and loving" God for no other reason than your love.
- Many of our hymns come from scripture. The scripture reference is on the page of the hymn, and there is also a scripture index in the back of the hymnal.
- One of the indexes in the back of the hymnal lists hymns by the authors. Charles Wesley was a prolific hymn writer. See how many of his hymns are in our hymnal.
- Doxologies are short hymns of praise. The one we use ("Praise God from Whom All Blessings Flow") was written in 1674 as the thirteenth stanza of a hymn.
- The *Gloria Patri,* ancient song of praise, was sung as early as the fourth century. The words are Latin for "Glory be to the Father."
- The psalms were the hymns of Jesus' day. Many of Charles Wesley's hymns were considered radical for his day. Some of them even used pub tunes of his day.
- The psalms were the hymns of the Hebrews. We use them in our worship in many ways. Besides being read from the pulpit, we sing them and use them as responsive readings. You may use the scripture index in the back of the hymnal to find various psalms.
- The closing hymn is our way of responding to God's call. Look at the words as your response to God with your dedication to action.

- The closing hymn usually challenges us to go into the world, changed by our encounter with God and the scripture.

Lights
- Candles were used in early Christian services primarily for the purpose of light by which to read. Today we recognize candles as a symbol of Christ bringing light into a world of darkness.
- Two candles on the altar or communion table remind us that Jesus was both human and divine.
- The tradition of an acolyte comes from the days when Christians worshiped in the catacombs in secret. The acolyte took the light ahead of them. Without that light they could not find their way. This also symbolized the light of Christ leading the way.
- The acolyte brings light into the sanctuary to remind us of Christ's presence. When it is taken out, we remember that we take Christ with us into the world.

Liturgy
- We call the form that we use in a worship service "liturgy," which means "The work of the people." Clergy and laypersons are "people."

Narthex
- The entrance room to our sanctuary is called a narthex. It helps us to make the transition into a spirit of worship and reminds us to prepare for worship.

Nave
- We call the section of the church building where the congregation sits the "nave." This stems from the Latin word for ship, *navis*. The ship or boat is the symbol for the church. The church helps us to sail safely across the rough seas of life.

Offering
- Some sort of worship experience where we offer thanks has been a part of most religions. In ancient times the offerings or sacrifices that were offered at such times were thought to

appease the gods and make for better crops. Today we understand the scientific elements of weather and their effect on crops, but we still have a deep need for giving thanks.

- The offering is a symbol of dedicating ourselves to God by returning some of what God has given us.
- The ushers bring our offerings to the front, not only to symbolize our giving of our money gifts but also to symbolize our giving of ourselves to God. We stand to affirm these actions.

Passing the Peace

- We can worship when we are alone, but in our corporate (or congregational) worship it is important to relate to other Christians. We cannot do that without knowing them. This is why we have a time of greeting in the service. This reflects the early church custom of "Passing the Peace."

Pews

- Our pews are arranged in a semi-circle, encouraging the community of our church fellowship.

Robes

- One of the robes worn in worship, the academic robe, came from the uniform of scholars in medieval universities.
- The alb, one of the robes worn in worship, was part of the everyday dress worn by Roman men and women prior to 400 C.E. The name means "white" in Latin.
- The stole, worn by ordained persons, was developed from the silk scarf worn by ancient Roman officials as a badge of their office.

Sacraments

- The word *sacrament* literally means "sacred moment"—a time when humans come in contact with the divine. Most Protestant churches recognize two sacraments, baptism and communion.

Sanctuary

- The architecture of churches usually includes high ceilings in the sanctuary, symbolizing our reaching upward to God. We recognize that God is not only above us, but all around us too.

- The word *sanctuary* means "a safe place" or "a holy place." Our sanctuary is a safe place for all people. We try to create an atmosphere of welcome.
- Some sanctuaries are designed in the shape of a cross, with the chancel at the top and two transepts (wings) on either side. This symbolizes the cross on which Christ died.

Sermon

- As you listen to the sermon, keep these questions in your mind: How is the preacher trying to make the scripture relate to your life? What do you want to happen in your life? What is the scripture saying to you specifically?
- In the sermon, the preacher speaks *for* God, *from* the scriptures, *by* the authority of the church, *to* the people.

Sunday

- In Jesus' day the people came together to worship on the day that is now Saturday. We use Sunday because that is the day of Christ's resurrection.
- We think of Sunday as a "mini-Easter," when we remember the resurrection.

Symbols

- After each service, altar flowers are taken to the sick. In this way we carry the risen Christ into the homes of those who could not be with us on Sunday.
- We often use plants to decorate our sanctuaries. The vegetation on the earth sustains us and renews the earth. Through the humus of plants, the soil is renewed. So we are renewed through the life of Christ.
- Any part of the architecture or furnishings that has eight sides can represent the idea of the Lord's day as the eighth day—a time outside of ordinary time, recalling Jesus' resurrection and anticipating his coming again.
- Any symbol with four units can remind us of the four gospels (Matthew, Mark, Luke and John). Our tables that hold our

flowers and the baptismal font have four corners. Use these to remind you of the gospels.

- Any symbol with three points or units can remind us of the Trinity, the three ways that we relate to God: as our creator/ parent, in a human experience, and within us.
- Banners have been used in church buildings since ancient times. Our banners remind us of the Christian seasons, but the cross is still our central symbol.
- Flowers in our sanctuary do more than decorate the chancel area. They remind us of the resurrection and indicate new life. We use live flowers to indicate this.
- The altar table under the empty cross is central in our sanctuary, indicating God's presence as our central focus.
- The communion table or altar symbolizes God's presence in the church building. It is the center of action in our worship, uniting us to God and to one another.
- The Bible is the center of our altar, recognizing that we hold God's Word as central in our lives.
- The color red signifies the flame of the Holy Spirit. Recognize this as you see red used in our sanctuary.
- The *empty* cross is central in our worship because it reminds us that we serve a *risen* Lord.
  The first stained-glass windows were used to help people (who could not read and did not have Bibles) to remember the Bible stories.
- The letters *IHS* on paraments stand for the monogram for Jesus Christ. Some claim the symbol is an abbreviation for Latin words that mean "Jesus, Savior of Men." Others believe it means "I (Christ) have suffered." Actually, the monogram is the first three letters of the Greek word for Jesus.
- The light behind our cross symbolizes Christ as the light of the world. We can recognize that Christ overcame death, the cross, for us.
- The pastors go out of the sanctuary ahead of the congregation, symbolizing their leadership in taking Christ into the community.

Worship

- Worship is like a drama. God is the audience, those leading worship (pastors, choirs, musicians, etc.) are the prompters, and the people in the congregation are the actors.
- Early Christians began worshiping on Sunday instead of the Hebrew Sabbath (or Saturday) because the resurrection of Christ was on Sunday.
- Our order of worship usually follows a traditional pattern: The Entrance, Proclamation and Response, Thanksgiving and Communion, and Sending Forth.
- The Christian practice of gathering in church buildings to worship God comes from the Hebrew synagogues. The term *synagogue* literally means gathering or assembly.
- The word *worship* was originally *weorthscripe* and later was *worthship*. Worship recognizes the worth of God in our lives.
- Worship is a dialogue. At times we talk to God, and at times God talks to us. Sometimes the worship leaders and choir "talk for us" to God through their words, and sometimes they "talk for God" to us through their words. Listen to the words and determine when this happens.
- The traditional 11:00 a.m. hour of worship came about during our agricultural era. It took that amount of time for a family to take care of the daily chores with animals and get ready and travel to church, which was sometimes a good distance away.
- The worship service is a model of how we should relate to God and to others throughout the week. In this manner, all of life should be worship, no matter where we are or what we are doing. It's *not* just Sunday morning.

Seasons of the Christian Year

Advent and Christmas

- Today begins a new church year in the Christian calendar. We celebrate a cycle during the year in order to make Christ more real and fresh each year. During the Advent and Lenten parts of the cycle, we use our senses to awaken our recollection of what Christ did for us.

- This is the first Sunday of Advent and the beginning of a new Christian year. As we decorate our churches and homes to remember Christ's birth, be aware of these ways that we remind ourselves of this significant event. Evergreens symbolize new life as well as life that does not die. Red symbolizes the drops of blood that Christ shed when he died for us. The circle of the Advent wreath reminds us of God's eternal love.

- The term *Advent* means "coming." Advent is our liturgical season including the four Sundays prior to Christmas Day. It is a time for waiting and preparation. The Christian church first began this celebration in the middle of the sixth century.

- Purple was a rare dye and very expensive in early Christendom; therefore it became a symbol for royalty. Purple, as the liturgical color for Advent, represents Christ as our king.

- The lights on the Christmas tree remind us that Christ has come as a light to a troubled world. We are also reminded that we are to be lights to those who need hope in this world.

- As the evergreen stays green during the hard times of the year, God's love is forever with us, even in the winters of our lives.

- The red poinsettias and bows represent the ultimate sacrifice, when Jesus gave up his life rather than sacrifice his beliefs.

- In the King James Version of the Christmas story Christ is referred to as the dayspring (Lk. 1:78b). This term means the start of a new day, or the opening of a new era.

- The liturgical color for Christmas is white for purity. We use that color from Christmas Eve until Epiphany, January 6.

- (*Use on the Sunday after Christmas.*) The actual Christmas Season of the church year began December 25 and extends to January 6. Continue to greet your friends with a wish for Christmas! Wreaths are placed in our sanctuary to remind us that, like a circle, God's love has no beginning and no end. The use of wreaths on our doors at home can signify that the meaning of Christmas is forever in our hearts, with no beginning and no ending.

- (*Use on a Sunday after Christmas.*) According to the liturgical calendar, we are now in the Christmas season. This season runs from Christmas Eve until Epiphany, January 6. The twelve days of Christmas include the days in between.
- (*Use on the first Sunday in January.*) This is the beginning of a new year. Look for something in worship that you can experience anew. Look at the world around you with new eyes and greet the people you encounter as if you were seeing them with new eyes, really seeing things from their point of view.

Epiphany

- Epiphany (January 6) celebrates the coming of the wise men with their gifts for the Christ Child. The Bible gives no reference to the number of wise men who came to see Jesus. Three gifts were recorded.
- The liturgical season after Epiphany lasts until Ash Wednesday and the beginning of Lent. The color for this season is green, symbolizing growth and hope.
- We celebrate Epiphany on January 6 or the Sunday after that date. This is the celebration of the coming of the wise men to visit the Christ Child. This event reminds us that Christ is for peoples of all nations. It is a time of centering on how we can show Christ to others.

Lent

- This Wednesday is the beginning of Lent, our time of preparing for the celebration of Easter. Lent begins with "Ash Wednesday" and includes the forty days before Easter, not including Sundays, which are considered "small Easters" during that time.
- We use ashes on Ash Wednesday to remind us that each of us needs the cleansing power of God.
- Ashes on Ash Wednesday remind us that God can take our sins and wrongdoings and destroy them as ashes.

- The liturgical color for Lent is purple, representing royalty and penitence. In preparing to meet our King we recognize ourselves as unworthy and in need of repentance. Therefore, purple reminds us to take inventory of ourselves in preparation for Easter.

Holy Week and Easter Sunday

- On Palm Sunday we celebrate Jesus' entering Jerusalem. When kings came in war they rode a horse. When they came into a city in peace they rode an ass. By his actions, Christ came into Jerusalem as a king in peace.
- Palms are used to remember Christ's entrance into Jerusalem on the Sunday before his crucifixion. The palm was handy in Palestine as a quick way to celebrate. This is the last Sunday we will use purple, the color for Lent.
- The dried bulb of the Easter lily represents Christ's death, and the glorious bloom of the lily symbolizes Christ's resurrection.
- In early Christendom Easter Sunday was the primary day of celebration in the year. New converts were baptized at the early dawn on that day.
- (*Use on a Sunday after Easter Sunday.*) We continue with the liturgical color white after Easter Sunday until Pentecost. The season of Easter goes from Easter Sunday to Pentecost. It is appropriate to greet persons with Easter wishes during this time!
- Christians are Easter people. For us every Sunday is Easter Day, a day to celebrate Christ alive!

Pentecost

- Today, Pentecost, marks the time when the Holy Spirit came to the disciples. You can read about it in Acts 2:1–13. The liturgical color for Pentecost is red.
- Pentecost is sometimes called the birthday of the church. This is the time when the Holy Spirit came to the disciples.
- The seasonal color for Pentecost is red, indicating the flame of the Holy Spirit.

Other Special Days

All Saints' Day—Many Christians see Halloween as the dark side of a holiday, symbolizing life without Christ. All Saints' Day (November 1) is the bright side, symbolizing those persons who lived in the past and those living today who follow Christ.

Most Protestant churches consider as saints all those who follow Christ, rather than only those determined so by an official church body.

Bible Presentation—We recognize our children by presenting Bibles to them on this special day. The Bible is presented to the parent(s) first and the parent(s) then present(s) it to the child because the parent has responsibility, with the help of the church, for sharing faith with the child.

Confirmation—This is a time when persons who have made a study of what it means to be a Christian, and who now confirm the vows taken for them at their baptism, are recognized as full members of the church. It is not a "graduation," but actually a *beginning* of a life dedicated to Christ and a life of study in order to follow God's calling in every way.

Reformation Sunday—During the sixteenth century, the church doors were used as a community bulletin board. On October 31, 1517, Martin Luther posted his statements that began the Protestant Reformation.

Thanksgiving—Thanksgiving should be a time of worship as well as celebration. Our biblical roots extend to Old Testament days when Hebrews celebrated three feasts of thanksgiving: Passover (release from slavery in Egypt); Pentecost (feast of first fruits); and Feast of Tabernacles or Booths (also called *Sukkoth* or ingathering, an eight-day end of fall harvest festival).

Trinity Sunday—Today is Trinity Sunday, recognizing the way that we celebrate God in three persons, revealed to us as our creator or parent, as in human form through Jesus, and as the Holy Spirit or God within us.

Worldwide Communion—The first Sunday in October is celebrated as Worldwide Communion Sunday. With Christians everywhere celebrating communion, we recognize our unity in Christ throughout the world.

This Sunday we celebrate Worldwide Communion with Christians throughout the world. This is a good opportunity to reflect on our role in the community around us as well as throughout the world.

COLORS AND SYMBOLS

This listing of special colors and symbols is in no way complete, but it will give you some suggestions. Some of the meanings of the symbols come from legends, and some remind us of different aspects of Jesus' life. Whether legend or real, they have the potential of reminding us of Christ. Use them in creative ways as you celebrate the Christian seasons, and be sure that the congregation is aware of their meanings.

Advent and Christmas

COLORS

Advent	purple	Royalty of Christ
	blue	Hope
Christmas	white	Purity
	gold	Royalty

SYMBOLS

angel	Angels who told of Christ's birth
bells	Celebrating Christ's coming
candles	Christ as light to a dark world
evergreens	God's love is everlasting.
manger	Christ's birth for all people
trumpets	Heralding Christ's coming
wreath	Eternal love of God

Epiphany and the Season after Epiphany

COLORS

green	Growth

SYMBOLS

crowns	Wise men's visit
dove	Christ's baptism
shell	Christ's baptism
star	Wise men

Lent, Holy Week, and Easter

COLORS

Lent	purple	Penitence
Easter	white	Purity

SYMBOLS

ashes	Our mortality and sorrow and repentance
basin and towel	Jesus' washing feet at Last Supper, servanthood
bread and cup	Christ's body and blood and Last Supper he had with disciples
butterfly	Resurrection (chrysalis represents tomb)
cock	Peter's betrayal (warns us to be loyal to Christ)
coins	Judas' betrayal of Christ
cross (empty)	Christ's resurrection
crown of thorns	Christ's suffering and humiliation
crucifix	Christ's sacrifice on cross
donkey	Jesus' riding into Jerusalem on Palm Sunday on a donkey
dogwood	Blossom in form of cross, legend that dogwood was a tall and straight tree until used as Jesus' cross

Easter lily	Bulb that appears to be dead comes to life.
eggs	Renewal of life and resurrection. In early days eggs were only dyed red to symbolize the blood of Christ.
fish	Greek letters for fish are first letters in "Jesus Christ, Son of God, Savior." Jesus told us to be "fishers of people."
lamb	Used for sacrifice. Christ sacrificed his life for us.
lantern	Soldiers used lanterns and torches when they arrested Jesus.
light	Christ's triumph over darkness (death)
nails	Nails driven into Jesus' hands and feet
palms	Jesus' ride into Jerusalem
passion flower	Five stamen represent five wounds; rays represent halo and divinity; leaf shaped like a spear.
pelican	Legend of pelican piercing breast with beak to feed young in times of crisis. Pelican catches fish, and Jesus told us to be "fishers of people."
robe and dice	Soldiers gambled over Jesus' robe.
rope	Used to bind Jesus
sand dollar	Four holes on shell represent four nail holes in Christ's hands and feet, and larger hole represents spear hole. On one side is the design of an Easter lily. The bones inside center of sand dollar are in the shape of doves.

seed	What appears to be dead comes to life.
stone	The stone over the door of the tomb that was rolled away

Pentecost

COLORS

red	Flame of Holy Spirit

SYMBOLS

boat	Church
curled lines	Rush of wind—Holy Spirit
dove	Holy Spirit
flame	Holy Spirit
rainbow	Holy Spirit

Ordinary Time or the Season after Pentecost

COLORS

green	Growth

SYMBOLS

leaves/plant	Growth of church
cross above globe	Christ's message to all the world

Other Special Days

TRINITY SUNDAY

symbols with 3 parts	Trinity

ALL SAINTS' DAY

hand with rays	God's blessings for all saints

—APPENDIX 3—

HANGING OF THE GREENS[1]

Here's a new twist for Sunday morning. It takes very little time during the corporate worship because you weave it into your regular order of worship, and people of all ages have opportunity to participate. Here's how one congregation set it up. Adjust it according to your usual litany of worship.

Leader: (after prelude): The prophet Isaiah wrote, "Prepare the way of the Lord." Let us prepare our worship area as we prepare our hearts for the coming of Christ.
(*Dim the lights.*)

CHORAL INTROIT (OPTIONAL)

Leader: The world sat in darkness, waiting for the light.

All: Our Lord, we await your coming. We recognize our need for your forgiveness and your love.
(*Brief silence for personal reflection*)

CHOIR: "Morning Has Broken" (*As the choir sings, the tree lights are lit.*)

PROCESSIONAL HYMN "Joyful, Joyful, We Adore Thee"
(*Lights are raised. Congregation stands.*)

CALL TO WORSHIP (*During this reading garlands are brought up the aisles and hung as planned.*)

---

[1]Delia Halverson, *Nuts & Bolts of Christian Education* (Nashville: Abingdon Press, 2000), 89.

Leader: God placed vegetation on the earth to sustain us and to renew the earth. Our plants give us food and shelter, and through their humus the soil is renewed.

All: Thank you, God, for your plan for renewed life. Thank you for Christ, who gives us new life.

Leader: As the green plants take in carbon dioxide and give off oxygen, the air on which we depend is renewed.

All: We come to this Advent season anticipating the renewal of your covenant through Christ.

Leader: As the evergreen tree is forever green, so we know that we can depend on God's love forever. We also know that through Christ's life we can experience life eternal.

All: As you give us eternal life, we pledge our constant love and service to you.

PLACEMENT OF WREATHS (*After reading, special music or a hymn may be sung as wreaths are completed.*)

Leader: The circle has no beginning and no end. God's love also has no beginning and no end. The red bows represent the ultimate sacrifice, when Jesus gave his life for us.

LIGHTING THE ADVENT CANDLE

CHILDREN'S MOMENT (*Invite children to come to the front for Advent Affirmation of Faith and explanations of the chrismons. The chrismons are placed on tree during the reading and anthem.*)

ADVENT AFFIRMATION OF FAITH

All: We believe in the one true God, almighty and greater than any king clothed in purple and gold.

Leader: In the ancient world, purple was a scarce color and therefore used by royalty. The color of Advent is purple, reminding us of the royalty of Christ. The crown reminds us that Jesus Christ is king of our lives.

All: We believe that God came to us in human form, as Messiah and Savior of all the world.

Leader: The shepherd's crook reminds us of those shepherds who first visited the Christ Child, and it reminds us that Jesus told stories of how God cares for us as a shepherd. The star reminds us of the night when angels sang and a brilliant star marked the birth of Jesus, our promised Messiah.

All: We believe in God, revealed in three ways but truly one.

Leader: The Greek letters on our tree represent various names for Jesus: Christ, Savior, Son of God. The first and last letters of the Greek alphabet, alpha and omega, remind us that Christ is with us from the beginning to the end.

All: We believe that Christ died for us so that we might live forever.

Leader: The various crosses remind us of that death.

All: We believe that Christ sent a Comforter to be with us, even after his death.

Leader: Jesus told us to be fishers of people. The fish represents Christians who kept their faith during the times of persecution. They used the fish as a secret symbol so that we might know about Christ today.

All: We believe that Christ calls us to follow him today.

GLORIA PATRI

ANTHEM

SCRIPTURE READING AND PRAYERS

PLACING OF CRÈCHE

Leader: The villagers of Greccio, Italy, in 1223, stood in awe as a dark, dismal cave came to life with the Christmas story. Saint Francis of Assisi envisioned this method of telling the story of Christ's birth with a live manger scene, complete with animals. Today we use the crèche to remind us that the story is real.

All: Thank you, God, for coming in human form. Through Christ we understand you better.

Leader: Although the shepherds and wise men came at different times, we include them both in our manger scene. This reminds us that Christ came for all of us, no matter what our circumstances.

Hymn "Away in a Manger"

Receiving of Tithes and Offerings

Leader: As Christ comes to each of us, we must share Christ with others. Through our gifts and talents we share Christ.

(For the remainder of the service follow the usual form. Any additional decorations may be added during the next week.)

WAY OF THE CROSS[1]

This series of centers is set up in separate rooms, with footprints on the floor leading from one room to the other. The information at the centers gives all direction needed, and so it is a time of quiet reflection and contemplation. Have hosts outside the first station to instruct people to space themselves and not enter the next room until it is empty.

You may plan for this to be open most of the day on Good Friday or another day of Holy Week so that families, individuals, or groups may move through the rooms at their leisure.

At each center there is a brief description of what happened at that time and opportunity for reflection. Reflection questions are suggested below; permission is granted for you to copy them and place them in appropriate locations. You will also want to display items that symbolize things in the story, such as money bag and coins for Judas, sandals for when feet were washed, crown of thorns, and so forth. Those suggestions are also listed below.

A Plot Unfolds

Judas plots Jesus' arrest

(Display: a brief description of what happened at that time, small cross draped in black, picture of Jesus, bag of gold coins)

- How do you see the Kingdom of God?
- Who is a part of the Kingdom?
- Is the person who lives in a small shack important to God?
- What about the person who treats you as if you aren't important? Is that person important to God too?

---

[1]Developed by Seekers Sunday school class of Cypress Lake United Methodist Church and edited by Delia Halverson. A version of this was previously printed in *Creative Ideas for Lent*, vol. 3 (Prescott, Ariz.: Educational Ministries, 1996), 35–38.

- Do you see people whom you don't know but whom you encounter in the grocery store or in the lunch room at school as individuals important to God? What about persons who cut you off as you're driving along the street?

A Parting Meal

Jesus washes his friends' feet, and they share a meal

(Display: a brief description of what happened at that time, pitcher, basin, towel, open sandals—communion elements at second location in room. The elements may be blessed ahead of time and taken independently, or you may arrange to have someone administer the elements throughout the day.)

- When did someone do something for you that you didn't expect her or him to do?
- What can you do for someone else that is beyond what is expected of you?

    Offer to care for a neighbor's child

    Tell someone that you like their choice of clothing

    Hold the door for someone

    Help neighbors clean their yard or do another family member's chore

    Let someone into the line of traffic

A Place to Pray

Jesus asks his friends to pray

(Display: a brief description of what happened at that time, bench in garden area, picture of Jesus in Gethsemane, clipboard for writing prayer requests, and basket of prayer bookmarks to take for use at home.)

- Think of Jesus here beside you, praying with you and listening to your prayers.
- What would you like to tell Jesus now?
- You will find a paper with prayer requests. Read the requests that others have made, and pray for them.
- Add any prayer request you may have and know that God listens, and God cares.

- We will also pray these requests at the service tonight.
- Do you have a special place at home that you go alone to pray?
- Decide on a time that you can set aside to talk to God each day.

The Enemy Comes

Jesus is arrested, and Peter denies knowing Jesus

> *(Display: a brief description of what happened at that time, picture of Jesus bound at wrists, leather strips, bag of coins.)*

- Look at the bag of coins. What in your life might the moneybag represent?
- Are there things you consider more important than Jesus?
- Feel the leather straps and have someone bind your hands. Imagine how Jesus must have felt.
- Remember that Jesus was aware of the physical troubles that lay ahead of him.
- Peter denied Jesus three times. What times do you find it hard to do as you know Jesus wants you to do?
- When can you help someone else to understand how you feel about God? Can you tell them about your church —or about some time when God helped you through a hard situation?

The Decision

Pilate washes his hands

> *(Display: a brief description of what happened at that time, picture of Pilate washing his hands, pitcher of water, basin, soap, and nice paper guest towels.)*

- Wash your hands slowly, remembering how often we all try to "wash our hands" of responsibilities.
- Ask God for forgiveness.
- Remember that Jesus has washed us clean by the grace of God.

They Mock Him

They place a scarlet robe and crown of thorns on Jesus and mock him

> (Display: a brief description of what happened at that time, picture of Jesus with crown of thorns and scarlet robe, large wooden cross propped on its side, crown of thorns, and bowl of vinegar with cotton swabs.)

- Look at the crown of thorns. Touch the points of the thorns. Think how it might have felt when the thorns were pressed into Jesus' head. You may even want to place the crown on your own head.
- When has someone made fun of you or said some unkind remark because of your belief or because you put your faith first? Next time this happens, remember that Jesus went through this experience too. You can make it!
- Feel the cross. Imagine how heavy it must have been. Would you have wanted to carry the cross for Jesus?
- When have you been asked to do something that seemed very hard?
- Next time this happens, remember Jesus and think of him as right there with you even though it's hard.
- The drink that was offered to Jesus was actually drugged wine, made by a group of wealthy women of Jerusalem as an act of mercy. The drugs would relieve his pain. However, Jesus refused the drink.
- The vinegar in the bowl is similar to the drink that was offered to Jesus. Use a cotton swab, dip it into the vinegar, and taste it.
- When have you suffered pain? Remember that Jesus understands our physical pain. When he refused the pain-deadening drug, he experienced what is said to be the most painful death that there is.

At the Foot of the Cross

A game of dice while Jesus says his last words; clothing was all that they thought was important

(Display: a brief description of what happened at that time, picture of Jesus on cross, crumpled white robe, sandals, and pair of dice. Beside the table, a large upright cross with a crown of thorns hung over the top and the last words of Jesus printed on paper, nailed to the cross.)

- Which is more important to you, people or a new car, a bigger home, a new toy or computer game?
- When have you failed to look for the good in someone else?
- Next time someone tells you, "Oh, you won't like that person," try to find something about the person that you can like. Remember, God loves the person.
- The world is much like that. We stand by while appalling tragedies are happening. The future of the human race is at stake, and all the while the playing of the commodity market goes on. *More* profits, *more* goods, *more* advantages, and we want it *now*. It is the latest chapter—*Will it be the last?*—in the continued story that began on Calvary, gambling at the foot of the cross.
- Read the last words of Jesus and pray: Dear Jesus, as you forgave those who crucified you, please forgive us for the many times we have wounded you by our thoughtless actions. Help us to follow your loving example as we interact with others. We rest in your promise that we will be with you in paradise. Amen.

It Is Finished

Jesus accomplishes his mission

(Display: a brief description of what happened at that time, at the chancel of the sanctuary, a large wooden cross laying on the steps, papers, pencils, hammer, nails.)

- Take a piece of paper. Write down any sins, fears, concerns, problems, or anxieties that you wish to get rid of and then fold the paper over.
- Use the hammer to nail your paper to the cross. Know that you have given Christ those things that you wrote on the paper. Christ helps us carry our problems.

- Pray: Jesus, our brother, the suffering of the nails must have been horrible indeed. Your hands that did so much good, your feet that walked to those who needed you, are now punished. You received little gratitude for the good you did. Why should we expect more for the good we do? Help us to give and expect nothing in return. Amen.

And We Are an Easter People!

Jesus promises to come again

> (*Display as they leave: basket with printed suggestions for ways to prepare for Easter Sunday and a schedule of services.*)

- We call Good Friday "good" because we know what happened at Easter. We know that God wouldn't let Jesus stay dead. We know that Easter made a difference in the world.
- Spend Good Friday in a reflective mood.
- On Easter Saturday have simple meals, make the house shine, and prepare yourself to welcome the risen Christ on Sunday.
- On Easter allow ample time to prepare for services and enjoy the exciting day.
- Remember that Easter Sunday is only the beginning of the Easter Season. Easter actually lasts for forty days, until Pentecost Sunday. Greet friends and family during that time by wishing them "Happy Easter!"

—APPENDIX 5—

THE DISCIPLES TELL THE STORY

Assign persons to read the following passages and to summarize the parts of the story that they will tell at the appropriate times. Some characters will have more than one passage to summarize.

The narrator begins the story, calling on others to "tell" what they remember from the assigned text:

> I recall the week that Jesus died. It's said that the disciples and Jesus had a meal together. **John**, will you tell us about the preparation for the meal? (Luke 22:7–13)

> Thank you, John. If I remember right, Jesus performed a common act before the meal, and **Peter**, you were disturbed with what he did. Will you tell us about it? (John 13:2–17)

> **Nathaniel**, will you tell us about how Jesus predicted that Judas would betray him? (Matthew 26:20–25)

> **Andrew**, you were at the supper; can you tell us about how Jesus used bread and wine to remind us of him? (1 Corinthians 11:23–26)

> **James,** perhaps you can fill us in about what happened next. (Matthew 26:36–46)

> **Peter,** will you tell us what happened when the soldiers came to the garden? (John 18:2–14)

> **Thomas**, will you tell us something about the trial of Jesus? (Luke 23:1–25)

Matthew, you later wrote about how the soldiers mocked him. Will you tell us about it? (Matthew 27:27–31)

John, will you tell us about the crucifixion? (John 19:16b–30)

—RESOURCES—

Calendar—Christ's Time for the Church by Laurence Hull Stookey (Nashville: Abingdon Press, 1996).

Christian Resource Institute *www.cresourcei.org* or *www.crivoice.org*

Christian Symbols Handbook: Commentary and Patterns for Traditional and Contemporary Symbols by Dean Moe (Minneapolis: Augsburg, 1985).

Introduction to Christian Worship by James F. White, 3d. ed. (Nashville: Abingdon Press, 2001).

Liturgical Design Institute (Annual institute in August, combining art, music, and liturgy)
> Scarritt-Bennett Center
> 615–340–7500
> 1008 19th Ave. S.
> Nashville, TN 37203
> spiritus@scarrittbennett.org

The New Handbook of the Christian Year by Hoyt Hickman, Don Sailers, Laurence Hull Stookey, and James White (Nashville: Abingdon Press, 1992).

The Special Days and Seasons of the Christian Year by Pat Floyd (Nashville: Abingdon Press, 1998).

The Spirit of Worship: The Liturgical Tradition by Susan J. White (Maryknoll, N.Y.: Orbis Books, 2000.

Symbols and Terms of the Church by Mark Bangert (Minneapolis: Augsburg Fortress Press, 1990).

Symbols of the Church, Carroll E. Whittemore, ed., rev. ed. (Nashville: Abingdon Press, 1987).